Universities and Regions

Bloomsbury Higher Education Research

Series Editor: Simon Marginson

The Bloomsbury Higher Education Research series provides the evidence-based academic output of the world's leading research centre on higher education, the ESRC/RE Centre for Global Higher Education (CGHE) in the UK. The core focus of CGHE's work and of The Bloomsbury Higher Education Research series is higher education, especially the future of higher education in the changing global landscape. The emergence of CGHE reflects the remarkable growth in the role and importance of universities and other higher education institutions, and research and science, across the world. Corresponding to CGHE's projects, monographs in the series will consist of social science research on global, international, national and local aspects of higher education, drawing on methodologies in education, learning theory, sociology, economics, political science and policy studies. Monographs will be prepared so as to maximise worldwide readership and selected on the basis of their relevance to one or more of higher education policy, management, practice and theory. Topics will range from teaching and learning and technologies, to research and research impact in industry, national system design, the public good role of universities, social stratification and equity, institutional governance and management, and the cross-border mobility of people, institutions, programmes, ideas and knowledge. The Bloomsbury Higher Education Research series is at the cutting edge of world research on higher education.

Advisory Board:

Paul Blackmore, King's College London, UK; Brendan Cantwell, Michigan State University, USA; Gwilym Croucher, University of Melbourne, Australia; Carolina Guzman-Valenzuela, University of Chile, Chile; Glen Jones, University of Toronto, Canada; Barbara Kehm, University of Glasgow, UK; Jenny Lee, University of Arizona, USA; Ye Liu, King's College London, UK; Christine Musselin, Sciences Po, France; Alis Oancea, University of Oxford, UK; Imanol Ordorika, Universidad Nacional Autónoma de México, Mexico; Laura Perna, University of Pennsylvania, USA; Gary Rhoades, University of Arizona, USA; Susan Robertson, University of Cambridge, UK; Yang Rui, University of Hong Kong, Hong Kong; Pedro Teixeira, University of Porto, Portugal; Jussi Valimaa, University of Jyvaskyla, Finland; N.V. Varghese, National University of Educational Planning and Administration, India; Marijk van der Wende,

University of Utrecht, The Netherlands; Po Yang, Peking University, China; Akiyoshi Yonezawa, Tohoku University, Japan

Also available in the series:

The Governance of British Higher Education: The Impact of Governmental, Financial and Market Pressures, Michael Shattock and Aniko Horvath

Changing Higher Education for a Changing World, edited by Claire Callender, William Locke, Simon Marginson

Changing Higher Education in India, edited by Saumen Chattopadhyay, Simon Marginson and N.V. Varghese

Changing Higher Education in East Asia, Simon Marginson and Xin Xu

Higher Education, State and Society, Lili Yang

The Governance of European Higher Education: Convergence or Divergence, Michael Shattock, Aniko Horvath and Jürgen Enders

Challenging Approaches to Academic Career-Making, Celia Whitchurch, William Locke and Giulio Marini

Universities and Regions: The Impact of Locality and Region on University Governance and Strategies, Michael Shattock and Aniko Horvath

Forthcoming in the series:

Online Learning Futures, Eileen Kennedy and Diana Laurillard

Universities and Regions

The Impact of Locality and Region on University Governance and Strategies

Michael Shattock and Aniko Horvath

BLOOMSBURY ACADEMIC
LONDON • NEW YORK • OXFORD • NEW DELHI • SYDNEY

BLOOMSBURY ACADEMIC
Bloomsbury Publishing Plc
50 Bedford Square, London, WC1B 3DP, UK
1385 Broadway, New York, NY 10018, USA
29 Earlsfort Terrace, Dublin 2, Ireland

BLOOMSBURY, BLOOMSBURY ACADEMIC and the Diana logo are trademarks of Bloomsbury Publishing Plc

First published in Great Britain 2023
This paperback edition published 2025

Copyright © Michael Shattock and Aniko Horvath, 2023

Michael Shattock and Aniko Horvath have asserted their right under the Copyright, Designs and Patents Act, 1988, to be identified as Author of this work.

For legal purposes the Acknowledgements on p. xiv constitute an extension of this copyright page.

Series design by Adriana Brioso
Cover image © Setthasith Wansuksri/EyeEm/Getty Images

All rights reserved. No part of this publication may be reproduced or transmitted in any form or by any means, electronic or mechanical, including photocopying, recording, or any information storage or retrieval system, without prior permission in writing from the publishers.

Bloomsbury Publishing Plc does not have any control over, or responsibility for, any third-party websites referred to or in this book. All internet addresses given in this book were correct at the time of going to press. The author and publisher regret any inconvenience caused if addresses have changed or sites have ceased to exist, but can accept no responsibility for any such changes.

A catalogue record for this book is available from the British Library.

Library of Congress Control Number: 2023937606.

ISBN:	HB:	978-1-3503-3758-9
	PB:	978-1-3503-3762-6
	ePDF:	978-1-3503-3759-6
	eBook:	978-1-3503-3760-2

Series: Bloomsbury Higher Education Research

Typeset by RefineCatch Limited, Bungay, Suffolk

To find out more about our authors and books visit www.bloomsbury.com and sign up for our newsletters.

Contents

Series Editor's Foreword	ix
Acknowledgements	xiv
Acronyms and Abbreviations	xv

1 Introduction — 1

2 The Problem with Regions — 13
- Regional inequality — 13
- Cities and regions — 16
- Regions and universities — 19

3 The Student Context: Recruitment and Graduate Outcomes — 29
- The national picture — 29
- The pre- and post-1992 divide — 31
- Graduate outcomes: the regional impact — 39

4 The Intersectoral Interface: Universities and Further Education — 47
- Relationships between further and higher education — 47
- The college/university interface — 49
- University/college network structures — 51
- The pre-1992 universities and the colleges — 55
- The management of the interface — 56

5 The Impact of University Engagement on Regions — 61
- Changing priorities in local and regional relationships — 61
- Universities' engagement strategies — 65
- Region, history and institutional mission — 72

6 Institutional Governance and Regional Strategy-Making — 75
- The changing shape of institutional governance — 75
- Institutional governance practice and regional engagement — 78
- Is there a governance deficit? — 82

7	**Regional Engagement and Universities: Some European Comparisons – Norway, Ireland and Germany**	87
	7.1 The regional factor in Norwegian higher education	87
	7.2 Regional policy and Ireland's technological universities: Balancing national and institutional ambition *Ellen Hazelkorn*	96
	7.3 Higher education and regional engagement in Germany *Jürgen Enders*	107
8	**Tertiary Education and the Role of Regions: The Case for Decentralization**	123
	The transfer from higher to tertiary education	123
	Lessons from European comparators	124
	The case for the decentralization of higher education in England	130
	University autonomy in a decentralized system	136
	Further education in a tertiary setting	139
	Assessing the value of regional engagement	140

References	145
Works Cited	147
Index	155

Series Editor's Foreword

Universities and Regions is the eighth book to be published in the Bloomsbury Higher Education Research book series. This series brings to the public, government and universities across the world the new ideas and research evidence being generated by researchers from the ESRC/OFSRE Centre for Global Higher Education.[1] The Centre for Global Higher Education (CGHE), a partnership of researchers from eleven UK and international universities, is the world's largest concentration of expertise in relation to higher education and its social contributions. The core focus of CGHE's work, and of the Bloomsbury Higher Education Research Series, is higher education, especially the future of higher education in the changing global landscape.

Each year this mega-topic of 'higher education' seems to take on greater importance for governments, business, civil organizations, students, families and the public at large. In higher education much is at stake. The role and impact of the sector is growing everywhere. More than 235 million students enrol at tertiary level across the world, four-fifths of them in degree programmes. Over 40 per cent of school leavers now enter some kind of tertiary education each year, though resources and quality vary significantly. In North America and Europe, that ratio rises to four young people in every five. Universities and colleges are seen as the primary medium for personal opportunity, social mobility and the development of whole communities. About 2.5 million new science papers are published worldwide each year and the role of research in industry and government continues to expand everywhere.

In short, there is much at stake in higher education. It has become central to social, economic, cultural and political life. One reason is that even while serving local society and national policy, the higher education and research sectors are especially globalized in character. Each year six million students change countries in order to enrol in their chosen study programme, and a quarter of all published research papers involve joint authorship across national borders. In some countries fee-based international education is a major source of export revenues, while some other countries are losing talent in net terms each year. Routine cross-border movements of students, academics and researchers, knowledge, information and money help to shape not only nations but the international order itself.

At the same time, the global higher education landscape is changing with compelling speed, reflecting larger economic, political and cultural shifts in the geo-strategic setting. Though research universities in the United States (especially) and UK remain strong in comparative terms, the worldwide map of power in higher education is becoming more plural. A larger range of higher education practices, including models of teaching/learning, delivery, institutional organization and system, will shape higher education in future. Anglo-American (and Western) norms and models will be less dominant and will themselves evolve. Rising universities and science in East Asia and Singapore are already reshaping the flow of knowledge and higher education. Latin America, South East Asia, India, Central Asia and the Arab nations have a growing global importance. The trajectories of education and research in Sub-Saharan Africa are crucial to state-building and community development.

All of this has led to a more intensive focus on how higher education systems and institutions function and their value, performance, effectiveness, openness and sustainability. This in turn has made research on higher education more significant – both because it provides us with insights into one important facet of the human condition, and because it informs evidenced-based government policies and professional practices.

The CGHE opened in late 2015 and is currently funded until October 2023. The Centre investigates higher education using a range of social science disciplines including economics, sociology, political science and policy studies, psychology and anthropology, and uses a portfolio of quantitative, qualitative and synthetic-historical research techniques. It currently maintains ten research projects, variously of between eighteen months and eight years' duration, as well as smaller projects, and involves about forty active affiliated individual researchers. Over its eight year span it is financed by about £10 million in funding from the UK Economic and Social Research Council, partner universities and other sources. Its UK researchers are drawn from the Universities of Oxford, Lancaster, Surrey, Bath and University College London. The headquarters of the centre are located at Oxford and there are large concentrations of researchers at both Oxford and UCL. The current affiliated international researchers are from Hiroshima University in Japan, Shanghai Jiao Tong University in China, Lingnan University in Hong Kong, Cape Town University in South Africa, Virginia Tech in the United States, and Technological University Dublin. CGHE also collaborates with researchers from many other universities across the world, in seminars, conferences and exchange of papers. It runs an active programme of global webinars.

The Centre has a full agenda. The unprecedented growth of mass higher education, the striving for excellence and innovation in the research university sector, and the changing global landscape, poses many researchable questions for governments, societies and higher education institutions themselves. Some of these questions already figure in CGHE research projects. For example: What are the formative effects on societies and economies of the now much wider distribution of advanced levels of learning? How does it change individual graduates as people – and what does it mean when half or more of the workforce is higher educated and much more mobile; and when confident human agency has become widely distributed across civil and political society in nations with little state tradition, or where the main experience has been colonial or authoritarian rule? What does it mean when many more people are becoming steeped in the sciences, many others understand the world through the lenses of the social sciences or humanities, and a third group are engaged in neither? What happens to those parts of the population left outside the formative effects of higher education? What is the larger public role and contribution of higher education, as distinct from the private benefits for and private effects on individual graduates? What does it mean when large and growing higher education institutions have become the major employers in many locations and help to sustain community and cultural life, almost like branches of local government while also being linked to global cities across the world? And what is the contribution of higher education, beyond helping to form the attributes of individual graduates, to the development of the emerging global society?

Likewise, the many practical problems associated with building higher education and science take on greater importance. How can scarce public budgets provide for the public role of higher education institutions, for a socially equitable system of individual access, and for research excellence, all at the same time? What is the role for and limits of family financing and tuition loans systems? What is the potential contribution of private institutions, including for-profit colleges? In national systems, what is the best balance between research intensive and primarily teaching institutions, and between academic and vocational education? What are the potentials for technological delivery in extending access? What is happening in graduate labour markets, where returns to degrees are becoming more dispersed between families with differing levels of income, different kinds of universities and different fields of study? Do larger education systems provide better for social mobility and income equality? How does the internationalization of universities contribute to national policy and local societies? Does mobile international education expand opportunity or further stratify societies? What are the implications of new populist tensions between national and global goals, as manifest for example in the tensions over Brexit in the UK and the politics of the Trump era in the United States, for higher education and research? And always, what can national systems of higher education and science learn from each other, and how can they build stronger common ground?

In tackling these research challenges and bringing the research to all, we are very grateful to have the opportunity to work with such a high-quality publisher as Bloomsbury. In the book series, monographs are selected on the basis of their relevance to one or more of higher education policy, management, practice and theory. Topics range from teaching and learning and technologies, to research and its organization, the design parameters of national higher education systems, the public good role of higher education, social stratification and equity, institutional governance and management, and the cross-border mobility of people, programmes and ideas. Much of CGHE's work is global and comparative in scale, drawing lessons from higher education in many different countries, and the centre's cross-country and multi-project structure allows it to tap into the more plural higher education and research landscape that has emerged. The book series draws on authors from across the world and is prepared for relevance across the world.

The CGHE places special emphasis on the relevance of its research, on communicating its findings, and on maximising the usefulness and impacts of those findings in higher education policy and practice. The CGHE has a relatively high public profile for an academic research centre and reaches out to engage higher education stakeholders, national and international organizations, policy makers, regulators and the broader public, in the UK and across the world. These objectives are also central to the book series. Recognizing that the translation from research outputs to high quality scholarly monographs is not always straightforward – while achieving impact in both academic and policy/practice circles is crucial – monographs in the Book Series are scrutinized critically before publication, for readability as well as quality. Texts are carefully written and edited to ensure that they have achieved the right combination of, on one hand intellectual depth and originality, on the other hand full accessibility for public, higher education and policy circles across the world.

Simon Marginson
Professor of Higher Education, University of Oxford
Director, ESRC/OFSRE Centre for Global Higher Education

Note

1   The initials ESRC/OfS/RE stand for, Economic and Social Research Council/Office for Students and Research England. Part of the original ESRC funding that supported the Centre for Global Higher Education's research work was sourced from the Higher Education Funding Council for England, the ancestor body to the OfS and RE. Research England continues to provide financial support for the research.

Acknowledgements

We wish to express our gratitude to the universities which allowed us to conduct interviews with relevant staff and to the staff both for the interviews given and for the data they made available during the pandemic. We hope that our use of the material will be helpful in providing insights into the relationships they have developed with their localities and regions. We would particularly like to thank our colleagues, Professor Ellen Hazelkorn and Professor Jurgen Enders for contributing authoritative chapters on Ireland and Germany respectively, and to Dr Mari Elkins for her advice on Norway, as European comparators to the development of UK higher education policy in its regional context. We are grateful to Helen Worger for making all our interview transcriptions these past six years, to Caroline Steenman-Clark for preparing the manuscript and to Dr Paul Temple for reading it and making a number of perceptive points. We would like to thank Alison Baker for her support for publication and her patience in respect to the timing of its completion.

The research has been carried out under the auspices of the Centre for Global Higher Education at Oxford (Director: Professor Simon Marginson). We would like to thank Simon for his constant support for the project and for the publication of its findings. The funding support from the Economic and Social Research Council and Research England (award numbers ES/M010082/1, ES/M010082/2 and ES/T014768/1) is gratefully acknowledged.

Finally, we would like to pay tribute to the contribution of our respective spouses, Joanne Shattock for her utterly invaluable assistance in IT matters and for reviewing the text, Peter Upor for providing critical family support during Aniko's working hours. The project is much in their debt.

Acronyms and Abbreviations

AoC	Association of Colleges (UK)
BAME	Black, Asian and Ethnic Minority student
BEIS	Department of Business, Energy and Industrial Strategy (UK)
BME	Black and Minority Ethnic student
CBI	Confederation of British Industry
CNAA	Council for National Academic Awards
CoD	Council of Directors
CSO	Central Statistics Office Ireland
DES	Department of Education and Science (UK)
DfE	Department for Education (UK)
DIT	Dublin Institute of Technology
EPSRC	Engineering and Physical Sciences Research Council
ESFA	Education and Skills Funding Agency (UK)
FDI	Foreign Direct Investment (Ireland)
FÁS	Training and Development Authority, Ireland
FE	Further Education
FEHEE	Further Education Higher Education and Employers (England)
FET	Further Education and Training (Ireland)
GCSE	General Certificate of Secondary Education
HEA	Higher Education Authority, Ireland

HEFCE	Higher Education Funding Council for England
HEIF	Higher Education Innovation Fund
HESA	Higher Education Statistics Agency
IFS	Institute of Fiscal Studies
IoT	Institute of Technology, Ireland
IPPR	Institute of Public Policy Research
LEP	Local Enterprise Partnership
MIT	Massachusetts Institute of Technology
NEET	Not in education, employment or training
NESC	National Economic and Social Council, Ireland
NHS	National Health Service
NIFU	Nordic Institute for Studies in Innovation, Research and Education
NOKUT	Norwegian Agency for Quality Assurance in Education
NSS	National Spatial Strategy, Ireland
NUTS	Nomenclature of Territorial Units for Statistics, EU
OECD	Organization for Economic Co operation and Development
QAA	Quality Assurance Agency
QR	Quality Rated funding awarded as the result of research evaluation
R&D	Research and Development
RDA	Regional Development Agency
REAP	Regional Entrepreneurship Acceleration Programme
REF	Research Excellence Framework

RSF	Regional Skills Fora (Ireland)
RTC	Regional Technical College, Ireland
SME	Small and medium size enterprise
SNP	Scottish National Party
STEM	Science, Technology, Engineering and Mathematics
TU	Technological University, Ireland
UCAS	Universities and Colleges Admissions Service
UCCA	Universities Central Council of Admissions
UGC	University Grants Committee
UKRI	United Kingdom Research and Innovation
VEC	Vocational Educational Committee, Ireland
WEA	Workers' Education Association

Chapter 1

Introduction

The literature about universities and regions over the last decade has been dominated by the theme of the contribution that universities can make to the economic, social and cultural environments of their localities and regions. Most universities can make a good case for their impact on their region. The subject has attracted the attention of OECD (2007); its chief *animateur* in the academic sphere has been John Goddard (Goddard and Vallance 2013; Goddard et al. 2016). Goddard himself was the academic driving force behind the OECD study. Inevitably, universities and their staffs have not been entirely disinterested in their accounts, as for example *Making an Economic Impact: Higher Education and the English Regions* (Kelly et al. 2016) written for Universities UK. As Cochrane and Williamson point out, this literature tends to identify universities uniformly 'as key transformative nodes in a globally networked and market dominated world carrying messages of competitiveness and innovation as well as actively delivering technological change through forms of knowledge transfer' (Cochrane and Williamson 2013). This approach sees the universities as the key actors ignoring the environmental context but also making the assumption that the process of university-regional engagement is broadly common across institutions in the system.

Our approach is different in that it emphasizes the diversity of the institutional landscape and the different hand of cards that different categories of institution have been dealt or have developed over time. Moreover, it seeks to show how regions and localities are different and how this can influence the character of an institution as well as the constraints it imposes on the strategies it adopts, both for its own future and for the engagement process with its local and regional community. We thus regard the diversity of UK higher education and the highly differentiated character and economy of UK regions as critical factors in understanding the sharp contrasts in the inter relationships between universities and their regions and the opportunities they offer.

What we find is that the institutional higher educational landscape is extraordinarily differentiated, its determinants being far less the current regulatory framework than the geophysical location of the institutions and the context in which they were founded. The two were, of course, often closely linked. Thus, the nineteenth century 'civic' foundations were the product of the Industrial Revolution and the perceived need for scientific and technological innovation. They were sited in inner city locations and were steered in their initial academic mission by powerful local and industrial interests. They were not, like the United States Land Grant universities and colleges, brought into being on the back of national legislation. More important, their constitutions did not include a commitment to 'public service', a distinguishing feature of the Land Grant institutions (Sorber 2018). In 1957, however, thirteen institutions, containing all but one of the original 'civics', shared a £43 million grant from the University Grants Committee (UGC), an enormous investment at the time, to further develop scientific and technological disciplines. This heavily reinforced their already established leadership in these fields and, over the longer term, prepared all those institutions that had benefitted to form the heart of the future Russell Group (Shattock 2012). A second wave of civic universities, university colleges given full university status in the post-War years (though Reading received its charter in 1926) were not so fortunate in their selection for priority investment.

The new civics were succeeded by the foundation of the so-called 'New Universities' of the 1960s, the 'Seven Sisters', with Stirling and Ulster Universities added after the Robbins Report of 1963. These 'New' universities were required, as a condition of being funded, to have at least 200 acres available for development because the costs of expanding the civics on their inner-city sites were proving to be so high. This automatically located them on out of town quasi rural sites; they became 'campus' universities. As they were founded by the state and not by local interests (though their sites were given to them by the local authorities which had made the successful bid for a university) they tended to lack the advantages and occasional disadvantages of relationships deriving from close physical proximity to local government. In addition, because of the heavy investment in science and technology to the civics in the 1950s (as well as the costs of upgrading the Colleges of Advanced Technology, originally founded outside the university sector, to technological university status in the post-Robbins period) they were not financed for ventures into 'heavy' science. (Warwick, the only 1960s New University founded in an industrial area, was initially denied resourcing altogether for an engineering department.) These factors profoundly influenced the character of their development and distinguished them from the earlier 'civic' universities.

The polytechnics, on the other hand, which followed a few years later, were established under local authority control and, because they were created out of mergers of existing leading technical colleges, occupied multiple locations within urban environments rather than initially building afresh on greenfield sites. More significantly, they were not funded for research and, when given university status in 1992, they were disadvantaged in respect to the pre-1992 universities by their lack of a back history of dual funding (that is for the inclusion of research funding within their recurrent grants) and by their exclusion from the, by then, regular research assessment exercises. Thirty years later these disadvantages continue to be demonstrated in university ranking tables. They were, however, strong in technical and applied disciplines including some not taught at all in the pre-1992 universities.

Post 2000, a new cluster of institutional upgradings occurred as previously designated colleges of higher education, mostly former teacher training colleges, achieved university status. Sometimes known as the post-post-1992 universities, historically these were small institutions characteristically located on the periphery of urban environments and not in town centres. They had specialized in the liberal arts fields and had developed much less on the science side. In consequence, they lacked the scientific and technological subject infrastructure which would facilitate collaboration with science-based industry thus restricting their engagement with their local and regional economies to public sector activities such as nursing, policing, social care and social work and, of course, teacher training. They are sometimes referred to, disparagingly, particularly in England, as 'teaching only' institutions.

These facts about institutional location and the timing of foundation constitute the crucial environmental framework which forms the higher education institutional landscape. Our first concern in this book is to illustrate how the characteristics of these different categories of university have interacted with their regional environment and how regional economies and cultures have impacted on the universities' own development, conditioning their strategies and profiles to their regional surroundings. Our second concern is to consider the architecture of the higher education system and the extent to which regional interests should be involved.

Developments in Scotland and Wales offer some indication of the impact regions make. In 1992, when the UK government decentralized the governance of higher education to separate funding councils in England, Scotland and Wales followed by devolution to Scotland, Wales and Northern Ireland in 1998, there was scepticism in England at least as to the wisdom of moving away from a common national system and to the potential dangers of parochialism and local political interference. The findings of our book *The Governance of British Higher Education. The impact of governmental, financial and market pressures* (2019) do not support these fears or at least they demonstrate that any negatives are far outweighed by the positives: in Scotland there have been tensions between the SNP-led government and the universities over funding issues and an unwise legislative intervention over institutional governance arrangements, opposed by the universities, but there has been widespread support in Scotland for the abolition of tuition fees as being in line with Scottish tradition; in Wales, a substantial programme of mergers at further education college and university levels has foreshadowed the adoption of a tertiary education system much more in line with Welsh needs than a Westminster-centric system. In both cases the reinforcement of national identity has given added distinctiveness to the institutions and to the higher education systems without in any way weakening their international profile in teaching and research.

In following up this research we selected twelve universities as case studies for interview: two Russell Group universities, both civic universities with their roots in the nineteenth century, two other pre-1992 universities, both founded in the 1960s on greenfield sites, four post-1992 universities, all former polytechnics, and four post-post-1992 universities, two of which were former colleges of higher education and two others, one of which had relocated itself from being a post-1992 university in Hull to becoming a virtually new institution in Lincoln and the other, the University of the Highlands and Islands, which obtained university status in 2011. Ten of these institutions were in England and two in Scotland and one in Wales. Half of the universities we had already conducted interviews in and had drawn ideas from for the previous book. In each case, we interviewed the vice-chancellor/principal, the staff member most active in leading regional engagement and the member of staff, usually the registrar, who could provide us with student data. Where it seemed appropriate, we extended our interviews to further members of staff. In addition, we interviewed policymakers in all three nations.

The UPP report *Truly Civic: Strengthening the connection between universities and their places* rightly says that 'universities have lost some of their tangible connection to their place' and that 'UK policy has been relatively territorially agnostic for many years' (UPP 2019: 7). We hope that our study will draw the attention of policymakers both to the extent that the regional environment shapes the character of institutions and that their ability to respond to central initiatives in respect to regional regeneration is profoundly affected by the diversity of their history and location. One theme which runs through the literature of regional engagement as well as through policy discourse and is used rather undiscriminatingly in the UPP report is that universities act as 'anchor institutions' in their local communities. The concept, however, is not well defined and has become a sort of term of art. We, therefore, asked a vice-chancellor whose university saw itself as an anchor institution how he would define the role. His response, impromptu, which we believe to be an admirable summary, was as follows:

> 'I believe that it is the description of an organization that within its place, within its geography, has a longevity and a purpose and an impact that creates, if you like, some staying power, some stability for its community ... we can, at least in a relatively small city become a part of the place in the long term ... this is a place in the community in which higher education is part of the way the community works.' (1)

The essential message is that to be described as an 'anchor institution' a university must provide economic and social stability to a community which is in part dependent on it. Many universities would also legitimately argue that they contribute much more than just stability and are partnering civic or quasi government bodies to drive new activities or doing so themselves. Such universities might reasonably claim to be 'anchor plus'. A good example would be in a statement from a senior officer at the University of Leeds who in response to our request to define the anchor concept in the Leeds context said:

'to me it describes exactly what a university should be ... We are the University of Leeds so therefore for us to succeed, Leeds must succeed. So as an anchor institution we have to be one of the key things that hold in place what is Leeds and why Leeds is special. And we can do that only by working with our partners across the Leeds City Region. Ultimately, if we get this right many of our graduates will work in the Leeds region so we have a duty to make sure we instil in them a desire to stay in the region and pay back to it.' (2)

However, in this study we have not chosen to categorize any institution as 'anchor' or 'anchor plus' on the grounds that this might too easily obscure the very real diversity to be found within the university-regional narrative.

A recurring problem in the study is to define 'region'. On the one hand the UK has twelve administratively defined regions, but these are so heterogenous, and contain within them so many separate economic and cultural sub regions that they are not helpful in serving as a focus to define relationships with individual universities except in very general terms such as, for example, recognizing the distinctiveness of the university system in Scotland. A second definition might legitimately be considered in England to cover 'city regions' contained within the metro mayoralties. If a substantial devolution of public services from central government in England is to become a political possibility the 'regions' coming under the Combined Authorities of metro mayoral governance may become the *de facto* regions reflecting social, cultural, economic and essentially governance bodies for the collection of data and measurement of performance. So far, however, only ten have been created. We will refer to them loosely as 'city regions' though in fact the name reflects where the mayors are based rather than any restriction of their authority to city boundaries.

Finally, there are the 'regions' as perceived by the universities themselves. These do not cohere with either of the previous definitions and may sometimes reflect a student recruitment catchment area or the region which reflects geophysical characteristics such as transport and other connections which combine to create a kind of sphere of influence for a university. These 'regions' can be quite large, as in the cases of the University of South Wales, itself distributed over several campuses, or the Universities of Chester, Lincoln and Plymouth, or simply huge, as in the case of the University of the Highlands and Islands, or even quite small as in the case of the University of Gloucestershire.

In interviews, we invited each university to define what it saw as its region and in only two cases did this coincide with local authority boundaries; in another, the university defined its region simply as the city in which it was located. This has meant that quantitative comparisons, even if desirable, cannot be possible because the regional bases are so diverse but this approach has the benefit of showing much more clearly how regional characteristics affect university strategies and development.

We have already said that most studies of the relationships between universities and regions concentrate on describing what universities believe they are contributing to the relationship whereas we are seeking to turn the topic round and show how localities and regions influence institutions and frame their responses to them. But our research leads to a larger argument in respect of the limitations of centralized national decision-making and to a need to draw regional decision-making much more closely into the policy framework. This would not just improve the effectiveness of university-region engagement but would also add to the distinctiveness of the institutions themselves. Our studies of Scotland, Wales and to a lesser extent, Northern Ireland, have convinced us that there is much to be gained by a decentralization of policymaking. Our evidence suggests that institutional differentiation is much more the result of historical differences and inequalities in economic and social environment than of a conscious adoption of a particular institutional mission and strategy. Moreover, the way such strategies have often to be pursued could be undertaken much more effectively if coordinated and integrated with other regional policies. Realistically, this can only be achieved if steps are taken in England towards a devolution of powers which reflect something of the decentralization followed by devolution which was undertaken in 1992 and 1998 in respect to Scotland and Wales. To assist this discussion we have included a chapter (Chapter 7) of separately commissioned reports on different approaches to regional involvement in higher education in three other European countries (Norway, Ireland and Germany). The purpose of doing so is not to identify a perfect model but to use these accounts to broaden our policy perspectives on the role of regions in the conduct of higher education.

Any discussion of the interaction between regions and universities must confront the issues of 'levelling up' and the reduction of the economic and social disparities within regions. Here, the recognition of the impact of the geophysical and historic context of their origins are especially important in considering the contributions that universities can make. The UK Levelling Up White Paper (*Levelling Up in the United Kingdom* 2022) makes little direct reference to higher education but our evidence confirms the critical role which universities with different types of locations and different academic strengths can play in a levelling up process. This brings into focus the arguments to move to a tertiary education system in England, recognizing that this has already taken place in Wales and is in process in Scotland, which would itself demand a substantial decentralization to regions to be effective.

In Chapter 8, we connect these perspectives with a discussion about the need to change to a tertiary education system and the wider debate about the devolution of centralized policies to regions in England and the recommendations in general in the UK Government's Levelling Up White Paper (2022) about decentralization.

The full list of chapters is summarized briefly below:

Chapter 1 Introduction

Introduces the central theme of the impact of regions on institutions; summarizes the book's argument through brief chapter synopses; explains the research methodology; and comments on the contribution of comparative accounts of three continental European countries to understanding UK structural issues.

Chapter 2 The problem with regions

This chapter addresses the issues surrounding the diversity of regions and the contrasting extremes of economic and social wellbeing and deprivation that they exhibit and the differential impact that this may have on the universities within their areas, as for example between urban-based universities in major cities and universities located on the peripheries of smaller towns. It explores the implications for universities of government policies for capital investment in infrastructure, primarily in urban centres, as contributions to 'levelling up' as compared with the benefits of investment in human capital through widening participation from deprived communities. The chapter examines the implications through the position of twelve case study institutions and shows how differentiation imposed by regional characteristics must be taken into account at the same time as diversity deriving from institutional histories and disciplinary backgrounds. It goes on to describe how this can affect the style of regional engagement and the priorities accordingly adopted.

Chapter 3 The student context: recruitment and graduate outcomes

This chapter highlights the sharply contrasting comparisons between national and local recruitment for different categories of universities and discusses possible explanations and their implications for students from disadvantaged backgrounds. It shows how one major civic university, where evidence is available, had a recruitment pattern in 1938, and even in as late as 1954, virtually identical to that of a former polytechnic sited in a similar urban location today. Turning to graduate outcomes, the chapter argues the economic and social value of graduates, especially those from borderline or deprived communities, returning to those communities, as against seeking employment in more affluent communities elsewhere. It quotes evidence from one university in Scotland founded precisely for this purpose. The chapter sets out tables comparing recruitment patterns and graduate outcomes in the twelve case study institutions and suggests that the return of graduates to their domiciliary communities may offer at least as valuable support to 'levelling up' in terms of the human and social capital they bring as capital intensive innovation hubs in major cities.

Chapter 4 The intersectoral interface: universities and further education

The relationship between higher and further education has been under researched. We have been able to draw on the results of a project on the university and college interface which suggests that, on the basis of a 49 per cent response rate, 89 per cent of colleges and over 50 per cent of universities have joint programmes concerned with student progression, franchising and validation agreements (Shattock and Hunt 2021). Our case studies demonstrated how some universities have created networks of colleges which provide alternative sources of access to higher education particularly from deprived areas. Local colleges, close to local communities, thus act as partners in reaching out into communities which universities find it more difficult to engage with. The chapter argues that, as now in Wales (and as in prospect in

Scotland), higher and further education should be brought together into tertiary education systems. This would have implications for the current centralization of policies for the two sectors in England.

Chapter 5 The impact of university engagement with regions

This chapter describes university engagement strategies, distinguishing between research intensive and research active and teaching-led universities. It shows that research intensive universities with historically strong science and technology departments lean more towards private sector or large-scale public and private sector engagement while research active and teaching-led universities, historically founded with much more modest science and technology operations tend towards engagement with the public sector of the economy – nursing, healthcare, social work, policing – rather than in industrial or commercial fields. It also shows how critical an institution's location and the character of its region can be in determining these strategies and creating its institutional persona. The descriptions of institutional engagement projects emphasize how their diversity is a product of their history, location and regional environment.

Chapter 6 Institutional governance and regional strategy-making

The last decades have seen UK universities concentrating on the national imposition of research assessment, marketization and performance in national and international league tables. The lay membership of governing bodies reflects this change of emphasis with a decline in local representation and a marked substitution of members from outside their regions. The widespread recognition of the economic impact of universities on localities and regions has prompted a renewal of interest in regional engagement but governance mechanisms have not adjusted to the new agenda. Our evidence suggests that very large-scale regional activities are being undertaken on the initiative of universities with minimal oversight involvement from lay governors with local knowledge and experience. This is not to say that these activities do not appear to be, as presented, as both valuable and successful. But the chapter asks whether collaborative arrangements for particular projects with individual agencies like the Local Enterprise Partnerships (LEPs) is a sufficient guarantee of itself that such activities, which may be primarily self interested, contribute appropriately to a region's wider programmes of economic and social regeneration. What machinery exists to protect the public interest? What regional machinery is available to coordinate universities' regional engagement? Is there a governance deficit?

Chapter 7 Regional engagement and universities:
Some European comparisons

Three continental European case studies have been selected to serve as comparators to policies followed in the UK. The first, from Norway, shows how although the political system strongly favours a regional approach and has encouraged mergers of non-university institutions to provide equal university opportunities to those available in the major cities, the single attempt to vest machinery within universities to encourage collaboration with local and regional partners has not been successful. The second, from Ireland, illustrates how attempts to decentralize a Dublin-based, highly centralized system to regional decision-making have so far not made the impact intended but the mergers of regionally-based institutes of technology into multi-site technological universities opens a new prospect for addressing regional needs. The third, from Germany, presents a case where decentralization to regional governments, the Länder, with universities coming under their control, is a feature of the political system, but where the inherent state concern for university freedom and autonomy has tended to conflict with incentives for regional engagement which is viewed as a more appropriate activity for *Fachhochschulen*, now operating under the informal title of 'universities of applied science'. On the other hand, the principle of 'homogeneous living conditions' across the *Länder* means that the degree of inequality between regions apparent in the UK acts to minimize the levels of economic and social disparity.

Chapter 8 Tertiary education and the role of regions:
The case for decentralization

The final chapter sums up the lessons to be learnt from the experience of regionalism in Norway, Ireland and Germany. On the basis of our research evidence, we argue the case for England to move to a tertiary education system. A natural corollary of this is to consider how best such a system should be orchestrated taking into account the arguments on governance pursued in Chapter 6. Our conclusion is that greater decentralization is necessary. Ways and means are discussed in the context of national moves towards some form of decentralization of government functions to regions. This inevitably raises concern about the preservation of university autonomy as it did when decentralization and devolution took place to Scotland, Wales and Northern Ireland in 1992, and the dangers implicit are discussed. On the other hand, the benefits of greater decentralization, both to regions and to universities, are highlighted as offering a credible way forward in the light of the prospective demographic-led growth in student numbers and the recognition of the case for a greater integration of higher education institutions with the economic, social and cultural life in the regions. The UK Government is in the process of creating a new architecture for regional governance in England through combined local authorities and metro mayors, and the Levelling Up White Paper envisages a considerable extension of the current state of play. We believe that this offers, subject to necessary safeguards, an opportunity to decentralize higher education and create a new structure where tertiary education is more integrated with the economic and social strategies required in each region.

Chapter 2

The Problem with Regions

Regional inequality

A key to any discussion about the relationships between universities and their regions is McCann's statement that 'the UK has the greatest spatial inequality in Europe' (McCann 2019) later endorsed by IPPR North (Webb et al. 2022) and the Levelling Up White Paper (2022: para 1.2.1). The extent of the inequality can be stated in many ways but the literature on the diversity of regional economies confirms the extensive gap between the South and the North. A comparison of disposable income between the North East and London, for example, puts London at £28,000 and the North East at £16,000. The UK Competitive Index (Huggins et al. 2019) shows the top ten performing localities in the UK to be in London with the addition of Windsor and Maidenhead, while of the lowest, two are in the South West, four in the East Midlands, three in Wales and one in the North West. For every job created in the north just under three jobs are created in the Greater South East (IPPR North quoting Office of National Statistics data). In terms of regions, the Competitive Index shows Wales, the North East, Yorkshire and Humberside and the East Midlands, in that order, as being the lowest performers. The 2070 Commission emphasized these inequalities in the following terms:

> The lack of genuine opportunities in terms of access to good quality education, jobs, health services, perpetuates structural inequalities. Local levels of deprivation are reinforced by regional imbalances in economic development and structure across the UK. These limit the growth in wage levels and job opportunities as well as available resources for investment in services and infrastructure. As a result, inequalities in the UK are concentrated and persist in particular regions. (2070 Commission 2020)

The distribution of affluence is to a large extent mirrored in R&D expenditure with Oxford, Cambridge and its sub-region and inner West London, in other words the 'golden triangle', commanding 31 per cent of all R&D spending in the UK and 41 per cent of publicly-funded R&D. Another way of demonstrating this from a university perspective is that Quality Rated (QR) research funding awarded on the basis of peer-reviewed evaluation through the Research Excellence Framework (REF) shows that for 2018–19 universities in the South received 63 per cent of QR funding, those in the North 22.5 per cent and in the Midlands 13 per cent. Bearing in mind the academically perfectly defensible policy of research concentration, this translates into 68 per cent of QR funding going to the twenty-four university members of the Russell Group, representative mostly of the oldest UK universities – Oxbridge, the Scottish Ancient Universities and the first generation of civic universities – while only 13 per cent goes to sixty-three teaching-led universities – post-1992 and post-post-1992 universities. Ten universities received 48 per cent of the total QR monies (Day et al. 2019: 51), but perhaps the most instructive comparison is on the regional distribution of business R&D expenditure:

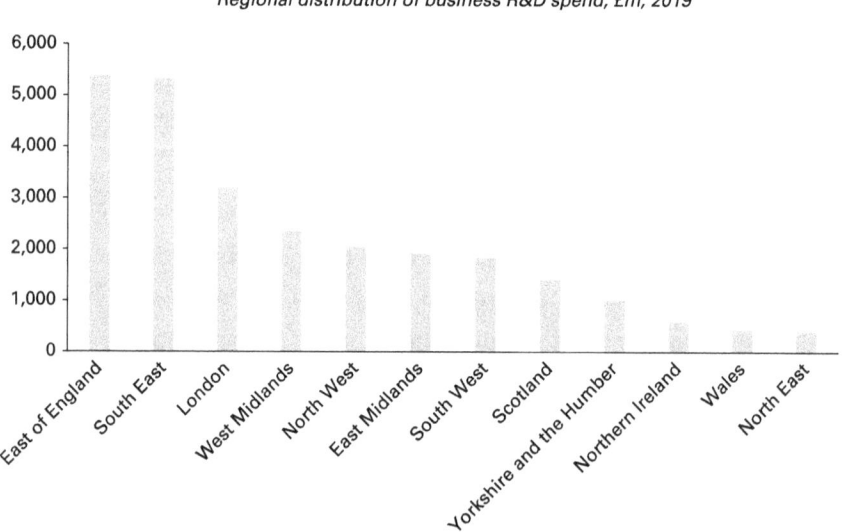

Figure 2.1. Source: HEPI Report, Chaytor, Gottlieb and Reid, Regional Policy and R&D, based on ONS data on gross domestic expenditure on research and development, by region, UK, 2019

It demonstrates, first, how unequal are the chances of universities in the bottom third to be able to compete with those in the top third in attracting research contracts from industry and second, the chart also functions as a proxy for the representation of historic investment amongst the twelve regions.

Analysis by region does not, however, tell the full story because economic and social disadvantage comes in pockets, some of them large pockets, in otherwise comparatively prosperous areas. Thus, the English Indices of Deprivation 2019 shows that of 317 Local Authority Districts, 260 have at least one of the 20 per cent most deprived areas within their boundaries (Ministry of Housing, Communities and Local Government 2019: 36). Map 4.2 of the Report shows how areas of multiple deprivation are spread in the North East, the North West and across Cheshire, the East of England around the Wash, and in the South West in Devon and Cornwall, all of which provide regional environments for universities in our study. This can be supplemented by evidence from the UK Competitive Index which covers Wales and Scotland as well as England. This shows that in a competitive listing of 376 localities, seven out of the bottom ten fell within the regional hinterland of a university. In the case of the University of South Wales, this included Blaenau Gwent in the South Wales valleys as the least competitive locality in the UK and Merthyr Tydfil forecast as having the slowest predicted GDP per growth capita in the UK.

These examples of the contrasts in the levels of prosperity in different parts of the UK are both a reflection of historical trends and of policy. The description of places 'left behind' can for example be misleading because some regions such as some of those in South Wales never benefitted from modern economic progress. Others are the direct result of de-industrialization, the closure of the mining industry or the collapse of the steel industry and of the supply chains which supported them. Such areas became socially depleted in terms of culture, education and above all financial investment which makes recovery that much harder to achieve. The eastward expansion of London represents a model for resuscitating impoverished industrial decline which can only be paralleled in other cities where an enormous concentration of financial resources can be brought together, but policies have also reinforced history. Coyle and Sensier have shown how past government grants for spending on infrastructure have skewed spending towards London and the South East because Treasury guidance and formulae rewarded past performance, widening the gap in productivity between London and the South East and other regions (Coyle and Sensier 2020). The successive application of research evaluation exercises which reward and penalize university performance since it was first introduced in 1985–6 has had a self-determining effect of concentrating research funding in a limited number of institutions many of which are themselves beneficiaries of being located in comparatively affluent environments. Since research prestige can be shown to affect student recruitment, high levels of research funding distort the student market and reinforce institutional recurrent funding through the recruitment of international students paying market-adjusted tuition fees; in other words, the rich grow richer (although for research intensive universities the costs of research intensity rise in parallel).

Cities and regions

In 2016, the Centre for Cities issued a report, *The Great British Brain Drain*, which contained the much-quoted recommendation that: 'The future economic success of the UK is increasingly dependent on the abilities of its cities to both attract and retain talent' (Swinney and Williams 2016: ch. 6). Its concern was the dominance of London in attracting new graduates away from the cities where they had gone to study for their degrees. It reported that London employed 22 per cent of all new graduates who moved from where they studied after graduation for employment elsewhere and 38 per cent of graduates who obtained first class or upper second class degrees from Russell Group universities as compared to 67 per cent of graduates moving away from Manchester and 86 per cent from Southampton.

These and other recommendations played strongly to a 'levelling up' agenda which was picked up in the Treasury Policy Paper *Building Back Better: Our plan for growth* (2021: CP 401) which argued that cities must be 'the engines for growth'. In doing so it set out an investment policy for levelling up in the following terms:

> Our city regions are critical for driving economic growth and long-term prosperity. We want to achieve dynamic regional economies with high value centres of excellence. The success of these are vital to the success of the wider region including increasing the opportunities available for the towns and communities surrounding these cities. (p. 71)

> We want every region and nation to have at least one globally competitive city acting as hot beds of innovation and hubs of high value activity. (p. 27)

Quoting rhetoric from the Prime Minister's Forward to the Policy Paper the aim was to 'level up the country so the map of our whole United Kingdom is lit up with competitive cities and towns that are centres of life – places people are proud to call home'. In a supporting passage in the Policy Paper the Treasury echoes some of the ideas contained in the Centre for Cities Report:

> Levelling up is about improving everyday life for people in those places [where they find themselves left behind]. It is about ensuring people can be proud of their local community rather than feeling as though they need to leave it in order to reach their potential. (p. 70)

The Policy Paper points directly to a strategy of investing in infrastructure in major cities and towns through a series of funds, a levelling up fund, a town fund, a high street fund, and a community renewal fund, leading to what are known as 'City Deals', in the expectation that their success will filter down to the communities on their periphery. Supporting the programme, it envisaged a major investment in skills training through further education and the new institutes of technology and higher education, essentially to facilitate the exploitation of research findings in economically productive R&D. The message is repeated in the Levelling Up White Paper (*Levelling up in the United Kingdom 2022*).

Building Back Better policies are already shaping those universities, located in the heart of the UK's major cities and with historically strong scientific and technological bases, which are in a position to benefit. These are clearly the older civic universities which over the years have built up large scientific and engineering schools. A prime example is the University of Manchester which is in the process of developing an Innovation District (ID) in the centre of Manchester with a property company, Bruntwood, and a financial services provider, Legal & General, both dedicated to the growth of science and technology-based R&D companies and other commercial ventures with close links to the university. The vice-chancellor, a distinguished scientist, is quoted as saying: 'We wanted to create the biggest city centre innovation district in Europe' (Staton, *Financial Times*, 3 June 2021). In fact, this is the second project the University has undertaken with Bruntwood, the previous venture being for an inner-city science park which already provides sites for some 150

R&D companies and research institutes. What Manchester demonstrates is the critical combination of location and the University's extended investment in science and technology over more than a century which makes this possible. It also demonstrates the attractions such developments can have for commercial property developers and financial investors – a glowing article in the *Financial Times* describes the vice-chancellor's reaction having travelled to Cannes to make a pitch for support for the ID project:

> We thought there would be quite a lot of interest … but I didn't expect them all standing down the side of the room … I was surprised by how many there were. The sovereign wealth funds, international pension funds … how big they were. (Hale and Bounds, *Financial Times*, 4 June 2019)

The project is indeed massive for a university-led development with expected expenditure anticipated to rise to £1.5 billion and the creation of 10,000 jobs in the next ten to fifteen years. It has used a site in its own ownership, the previous home of the University of Manchester Institute of Science and Technology (UMIST), which merged with the University of Manchester in 2004, and it plans to replace it with new and existing buildings which will contribute to changing the centre of the city. The presence of two other universities close by, the University of Salford and the Manchester Metropolitan University, the former a 1960s upgraded college of advanced technology and the latter a post-1992 university, produces a combined student population of some 100,000 which also impacts on city centre social and cultural life. The Manchester example can thus be seen as a realization or even a model for the policies in the *Building Back Better* Policy Paper; there can be no question but that it will shape the University's future. How far the transformational process will stretch, however, is more open to question. Already it is apparent that some companies, keen to move into the newly prosperous city centre, are closing down peripheral sites. Nor is it clear that the idea of cities and selected urban communities outside them will do more than produce a trickle-down effect on deprived communities in, for example, Oldham. Nevertheless, as evidence of how its environment can impact on a university as well as of how a university can impact on its environment, the Manchester strategy offers a validation of the Government's strategy in the particular circumstances of a city looking for regeneration and the presence of a long-established university with an exceptionally strong science base.

Regions and universities

Any description of the university landscape will show enormous diversity based on the history and context of the universities' foundation: a university founded on a greenfield site in the 1960s will look very different to a civic university originating in the nineteenth century, which again will look and feel very different to a university created from a polytechnic in 1992, and even more so to a former college of higher education awarded university status in the post-2000 era. This diversity is reinforced by the diversity of their actual regional location and the way that this has determined their development and ongoing strategies. In selecting our twelve universities for close examination as to their relationship with their regions, our first criterion was to seek to mirror the direct impact of the diversity of the overall UK university landscape but it rapidly became clear that historic and academic diversity was also rooted in the diversity of universities' regional hinterlands, the areas which they themselves see as defining their regional location. We have chosen, therefore, to base our accounts on the individual regions identified by the universities themselves rather than those conventionally adopted by outside agencies or authorities.

One immediate point of differentiation was whether the university was in the centre of a major city as the University of Manchester is, rather than on the periphery. Two of our case study universities, Leeds and Newcastle, have followed a similar pattern of urban engagement to Manchester's. Both grew from initial foundations in the nineteenth century in major industrial cities, and their academic profiles were targeted at science, technology and medicine: Leeds (as the Yorkshire College) was originally driven by local concerns about technological competition with continental Europe, Newcastle (as Armstrong College) by the need for medical education and the demands of the mining industry. Both are sited in the heart of their cities and near their civic authorities – in Newcastle the windows of the offices of the city's chief executive and of the vice-chancellor overlook one another. Both universities, like Manchester, are engaged in transformative urban redevelopment through the creation of innovation hubs which plan to draw on university-based research to generate economic renewal. Both might fall into the category of Innovation Accelerators envisaged in the Levelling Up White Paper as being characterized as offering high tech research-based support to their city regions via funding streams which combine national sources like the research councils and QR monies with regional and civic investment.

A third example, in Birmingham, offers a considerable contrast. Here we have a city in which the decision by Goldman Sachs to open a global software development site signals, in the view of the *Financial Times*, its establishment as an 'alternative to London' confirming its 'rise as a finance and tech hub' (Bounds 2021). Our case study university is not a high-tech scientific and technological one as in Leeds and Newcastle but Birmingham City University, a former polytechnic, which in its strapline calls itself the University *for* Birmingham to distinguish its role as it sees it, from the University of Birmingham which fits the historic model provided by Leeds, Newcastle and Manchester. The distinction to be drawn between the two universities is as follows: Birmingham City University is located right in the heart of the city with, like most former polytechnics, a number of sites scattered round the city centre; the University of Birmingham, on the other hand, is located in Edgbaston some three miles from the city centre. The University had opened as Mason's College in 1880 in the city centre with the object, as specified in its Foundation Deed, of providing 'systematic education and instruction specially adapted to the practical, mechanical and artistic requirements of the manufactures and industrial pursuits of the Midlands district' (Ives et al. 2000). But in 1900, when it received its charter to be the University of Birmingham, it received a gift of land from the Calthorpe estate to develop a new university site in Edgbaston to which it ultimately transferred (though it continued to occupy its city centre site until the 1960s). Although no one would doubt Birmingham University's commitment to the city and to the West Midlands, its location and its national eminence and national recruitment of students has enabled Birmingham City University to claim a special role as addressing the city's labour market needs in a way that Birmingham's internationally ranked Russell Group university would not claim to do. With a large majority of its students coming from the West Midlands, mostly as daily commuters, and an almost equally large majority of its UK graduates taking employment in the city, Birmingham City University is integral to the city's prosperity and rise in status. Without it, the University can claim that 'the city probably wouldn't actually be able to operate in terms of having its schools, its hospitals, its engineering facilities and also its arts in place' (1). Anticipating demographic growth in the city's eighteen-year-old population it intends to grow its local recruitment in concert. At the same time, the city's development and its burgeoning ability to attract high profile companies to locate in, it serves to shape the University's strategy: it sees itself and its future as a significant element of a very large and successful civic enterprise.

The University of East London, another post-1992 institution, offers a further example of urban living, but as the centre of a city region within the much larger context of London. Where Birmingham City University identifies itself with a single city domain, East London regards its engagement as first with the borough of Newham where the University's three campuses are located, and more broadly with the five boroughs of Barking and Dagenham, Hackney, Newham, Redbridge and Tower Hamlets which supply the majority of home students, 74 per cent of whom are from ethnic minorities. Historically these boroughs all contain pockets of extreme social deprivation: Newham suffers from acute child poverty and contains the largest foodbank provider in the UK. But London affluence is moving east: the Lord Mayor is moving his office to a site 100 yards away from the University and one of the University's campuses, the Royal Albert Docks, is part of the Royal Docks Enterprise Zone which promises to transform the area with investment in business parks, innovation centres and residential developments. From a situation where student recruitment fell by almost a third and the University finances became the subject of scrutiny by the Higher Education Funding Council for England (HEFCE), student numbers have revived and the University is in financial surplus. While in no sense abandoning its mission towards the five boroughs, the University is confident that its profile and range of activities will grow in concert with the future prosperity of the locality. As one senior member of the University's team emphasized in answer to a question about the University's strategies being determined by its location:

> 'Context is critical ... East London is a fast moving dynamic place in terms of infrastructure, in terms of spaces, in terms of demographics, and I think

that as they continue to change, then different drivers come into play as well, so it's not just about the transformation of those who maybe wouldn't have had opportunities before, it's also transformation of opportunities for those who want to change and develop new opportunities and skills.' (2)

As in Birmingham, urban development strategies drive university strategies.

Our next two universities, Gloucestershire and Chester, could not be described as being sited in 'fast moving dynamic' locations. Both have histories extending back into the early- to mid-nineteenth centuries, primarily as Anglican teacher training colleges academically orientated towards the humanities and liberal arts; both passed through college of higher education status (Cheltenham and Gloucester College, and University College Chester) to full university in the post-2000 second wave of post-1992 universities. Both are also located in affluent smaller sized towns with excellent academically orientated schools catering to the needs of a middle-class clientele which would anticipate their children achieving places at Russell Group universities. The universities' contrasting development following their transfer to university status, however, represents clear evidence of how the impact of their environment can act as a determinant of their futures.

When the Cheltenham and Gloucester College sought the support of Gloucestershire County Council for its university status bid it was made clear that this would be conditional on opening a campus in Gloucester. Cheltenham was a wealthy and attractive place to live, and Gloucester had need of regeneration and was economically depressed; the University now has campuses in both towns, in Cheltenham in a park setting, and in Gloucester on a down-town urban site. Gloucester was described by a senior member of the University as 'a sort of northern industrial town translated by accident into a rural mid-England shire' (3). As a second senior member put it:

> 'Cheltenham and Gloucester like to pretend that there are several hundred miles between the two of them [the actual distance is ten miles] and they have nothing to do with one another ... taken together they are quite an important centre, taken separately they are effectively two minor provincial towns.' (4)

The county, however, has many unifying characteristics: the LEP operates on a county basis as does the NHS structure, and a Gloucestershire City Region

Board, in the creation of which the University played a large part, all combine to establish a coherent economic and political structure. The vice-chancellor has regular meetings with the leaders of the Cheltenham Borough Council and the Gloucester City Council and the LEP's offices are on the Cheltenham campus. The University's strategy is based on this congruence of interests: 'our mission is to be the university of our place and an anchor for our place' (5).

Where Gloucestershire sees itself as serving a single county region, the region Chester has defined for itself is much more diverse enclosing Cheshire, Warrington and the Wirral to the north and west, and, to the south, Shrewsbury and the Marches skirting the fringes of Liverpool and Manchester. Parts of Cheshire are affluent and rural, but parts are industrial with a very substantial chemical industrial base. Ellesmere Port, only eight miles from Chester, is one of the most deprived areas in the UK where the University has established a science park with LEP and Department of Business, Energy and Industrial Strategy (BEIS) support, adjacent to the Stanlow Oil Refinery. It has a campus in Warrington where it is keen to expand student numbers and is abandoning the previous Padgate College campus, formerly validated by Liverpool University, for a town-centre site. It also has a campus in Shrewsbury. Unlike the single county approach of Gloucestershire, it has a close relationship with the Mersey-Dee Alliance, a regional strategic economic partnership, and the councils of Chester West and Chester, Shropshire and Warrington Borough, and with the Cheshire and Warrington LEP. What this reflects is the untidy diversity of the region where the University has chosen to position itself, away from its main Chester campus, in locations characterized by industrial decline and low participation rates, a transformation of its own profile from the middle class, cathedral-linked teacher training college from which it has grown.

The University of Plymouth presents a sharp contrast to Chester in the unequivocal definition of its region as being the South West stretching from the tip of Cornwall to the borders of Gloucestershire, but it is also very large – from Penzance at one end to Bristol at the other is half as far as London to Edinburgh – necessitating secondary campuses in Exeter and Truro. The University works closely not only with the Plymouth City Council but with three LEPs and five major hospitals. The region includes, in the Cornish, Devon and Somerset peninsula, some of the most economically starved areas in the UK in spite of a booming tourist trade; although there is a concentration of marine, offshore renewables and defence companies in and around Plymouth, 90 per cent of companies in the region employ fewer than ten staff. The University, one of the most research-active of the post-1992 generation of universities, has long established partnerships with the twelve further education colleges in the region and draws about a third of its home undergraduate population from this source. Through its relationships with further education and the validation services it provides it represents a unique contact with higher education for small deprived fishing, mining and farming communities otherwise cut off from the opportunities universities can offer.

A very similar picture can be painted of the University of South Wales in that its region, defined as the Cardiff capital region covering as many as ten local authority areas, represents the post-industrial part of Wales – 'where most of our campuses sit is where actually the hard graft of digging stuff out of the ground, making steel, that heritage [used to take place]' (6). What is unlike Plymouth, however, is that although the region has a name for economic planning purposes it is actually not at all clearly defined in terms of geography and institutional homogeneity. Whereas Plymouth moved smoothly from polytechnic to university status, the University of South Wales represents a merger constructed of the former University of Glamorgan and University College Newport with its headquarters in Pontypridd, which itself has three sub-campuses, and also campuses in Cardiff and Newport. This spreads it over a very diverse region and means that it can lack the focus which a single inner-city site like Plymouth's can provide. On the other hand, it has the benefit of offering close contact with the communities it seeks to serve.

The University of Lincoln provides a further contrast to the Chester, Plymouth and South Wales stories. Here, the University owes its origins to the Humberside College of Higher Education based in Hull which achieved university status in 1992. At the invitation of the city of Lincoln, keen to acquire a university to broaden its economy, it transferred to Lincoln over the 1990s and established itself as the University of Lincoln with its main campus in the centre of the city in 2002. From that point it was, as one of its senior staff described it, 'a long start-up' (7). Interestingly, the city authorities bypassed the local Anglican teacher training college with its strong cathedral links (now Bishop Grosseteste University) seemingly searching for a more economically enterprising organization which would impact on the local economy and on jobs. The University's initial engagement may, therefore, have been with the city of Lincoln, and in practice it has made a substantial physical impact on the city centre, but its presence, combined with considerable institutional leadership, has turned it into a regional university whose region extends from the Humber to the Wash embracing greater Lincolnshire and the East Midlands, all areas which justify the description of being 'left behind'. Animated by a vision to transform its region and working in consort with an active LEP for Greater Lincolnshire, the University has developed its regional profile in partnership with existing nodes of activity – Siemens for engineering, the Lincolnshire Co-op for pharmacy, hospitals in Lincoln, Boston and Grantham for medicine, the farming community for agri-robotics, the cathedral archives for mediaeval history, and a range of public services – so that its activities have been shaped profoundly by its regional community. The policy of 'working with the assets that you have' (8) has made the University something of a mirror image of its urban and regional environment. One measure of success can be adduced from its impact in bricks and mortar with nineteen new major capital projects completed during the outgoing vice-chancellor's twelve-year period in office.

The University of the Highlands and Islands in Scotland offers an alternative perspective on region. Founded in 1992 as the Highlands and Islands Millennium Institute, it became a full university in only 2011. Its region covers one-sixth of the UK's landmass and the University itself represents the integration of thirteen further education colleges and research organizations distributed over centres of population across a very broad sparsely populated and mountainous landscape. Although its headquarters are in Inverness, its teaching and research are carried out in the colleges (which also teach at FE levels) and research establishments; in respect to its Island constituents, it is very dependent on online teaching arrangements. Originally founded and developed with help from Highlands and Islands Enterprise and its predecessor the Highlands and Islands Development Board, its aim was initially to provide a way of retaining its young population in the region rather than seeing them leave for higher education in the urban centres in the south never to return, but increasingly its partnership with Highland and Islands Enterprise has made it a force in regional economic development. This is the only university in the UK to have been established in modern times specifically to meet regional need; unlike Lincoln it has administratively defined regional borders and is accountable to a 120-member Highlands and Islands Foundation, representative of the many communities it serves.

Our last two case study universities, Lancaster and Stirling, offer the sharpest contrast to the Highlands and Islands University. Both were founded by the University Grants Committee (UGC) in the 1960s against bids submitted by local communities. Both were sited adjacent to but not within small towns – Lancaster population 52,000 with 133,000 in its local authority district, Stirling population 37,000 with 94,000 in its local authority district – and both were located on attractive rural campuses away from the town centres; both are substantially residential. As one senior official from Lancaster said: 'We are a campus-based university, that is our whole brand, our whole product, sort of sales pitch' (9). In Lancaster's case, the LEP for Lancashire is not even sited in Lancaster but in the larger city of Preston some ten miles away. Academically, both are what might be described as 'dual intensives', that is universities that would claim to be both research intensive and to excel in teaching. In regional terms Lancaster, like Chester and South Wales, does not have a well-defined region but identifies it as a generic North West hedged around by major university conurbations in Manchester and Liverpool. Stirling is able, on the other hand, to identify itself with the Forth Valley (population over 300,000) but chooses now to regard its region as the central belt of Scotland 'but it's a very diffuse and dispersed region and it has some quite significant social and economic polarizations' (10). Like Lancaster, it has powerful competition with Edinburgh, Glasgow and Dundee only an hour's drive away. Neither university has a strongly industrial hinterland, and both are close to areas of serious economic deprivation – Lancaster in Morecambe and Blackpool and the Fylde, Stirling in Alloa and Clackmannanshire.

Both universities had initially concentrated on building up their academic reputations in order to compete with the older and larger civic universities but a decade ago recognized the importance of a regional agenda. In Lancaster, the University was viewed locally as 'the sort of university on the hill that was distant and isolated and, other than providing employment for some, didn't particularly engage with the local community and saw its commitment as global' (11); now its agenda is formulated much more as 'making universities relevant to their local communities' (12). Stirling 'did not have a great relationship with the local authority in Stirling', and they carried out their business 'within this beautiful walled campus state' but now they have a close relationship with all three local authorities within their region; now 'it benefits everybody in the University to be firmly anchored within the locality and region that we operate within' (13) and it can be claimed that 'we are an absolutely central community resource' (14). Both universities were at first isolated from their localities and regions by their locations and by the need to make their mark in the then traditional vertical structure of the UK university system; their campus style was attractive to students and staff alike especially when compared with the inner-city sites of some of their civic rivals. But now leadership, a recognition of the growing economic and social inequalities within their neighbourhoods and the availability of new sources of place-related funding together with market pressures has had transformative effects. Regional activities and concerns can be said to be reshaping both universities away from their 1960s model.

In all twelve cases, therefore, region, though often unacknowledged, has had a dominant impact on a university's development and the universities' own histories have determined their response. While at one level higher education is a global entity, as can be demonstrated in each of the institutions in our case studies, the shape of these universities is in fact intensely regional and local. When thinking about how they relate to their regions and localities it is important to recognize how the diversity of their contributions reflects the diversity in the strengths, and weaknesses, which they bring to the higher education system.

Chapter 3

The Student Context: Recruitment and Graduate Outcomes

The national picture

One of the most marked divisions between universities' relationships with their regions is the extent to which their student recruitment is based primarily locally or regionally or is essentially nationally based. In 1962, when the Universities Central Council of Admissions (UCCA) first opened its operations, it did so, not from any principled plan to encourage applicants to leave home to study at university but to rationalize the admissions process for universities so that with the restriction to five university choices, universities were protected from having to process unnecessary multiple applications. The impact of offering five choices, however, certainly had the effect of encouraging candidates to be more adventurous in applying to universities outside their locality or region. This was, without doubt, beneficial to lower-profile pre-1992 universities, and perhaps particularly to the new foundations of the 1960s which did not have a long back history or strong local image to draw upon. The creation later of a centralized polytechnics and colleges admissions system (PCAS) did not, however, have the same effect. Whitburn et al. published comparative material about polytechnic entrants in the mid-1970s, before the polytechnic service merged with UCCA to form the Universities and Colleges Admissions Service (UCAS), which showed that 50 per cent of polytechnic entrants had chosen to apply to polytechnics because their 'A' level scores were not appropriate to university admission. But Whitburn et al. published a separate table which showed that the parents of university entrants also had significantly higher social and educational characteristics than parents on the other side of the binary line (Whitburn et al. 1976: 5, Tables 5.3 and 5.4). A study by Donnelly and Gamsu for the Sutton Trust (2018) concluded on the basis of the 2014–15 applications season that there:

> are deeply entrenched historical differences in how different social classes experience and make mobility decisions about higher education. These fundamental differences . . . are underpinned by a system of higher education which still operates a binary divide which is spatial as well as social. There is a tension between universities which serve the majority of the working class commuting students and those elite universities that recruit nationally from more affluent families and are more isolated from their local communities. (Donnelly and Gamsu 2018: 25)

They show that although the majority of students attend universities less than about fifty-five miles away from their home address, 'three times more students in the lowest social class group commute from home than do so from the highest group (44.9 per cent compared with 13.1 per cent)' (Donnelly and Gamsu 2018: 4).

Donnelly and Gamsu and the Higher Education Statistics Agency (HESA) construct tables which show breakdowns of data of the percentages of students attending local universities but these are based on the twelve administrative regions and do not take account of the relationship between the number of the universities and the size of the regions. However, Whitburn et al. give some perspective from the mid-1970s about polytechnics, though detailed comparisons with Donnelly and Gamsu are not possible because they did not define the students' region of domicile with more precision than simply 'The percentage of [full-time] students whose home area is same as polytechnic area', and do not follow the standard regional definitions, excluding data for Scotland altogether. Nevertheless, they are worth quoting as providing some indication of the extent to which polytechnics were dependent on local as compared to national recruitment at that time: North East 59 per cent, North West 63 per cent, Midlands 46 per cent, South East 29 per cent, South West including Wales 62 per cent, London 40 per cent (figures based on full-time students at twenty-eight polytechnics) (Donnelly and Gamsu 2018: Figure 5.1). These figures are not surprising: polytechnics were established to meet local needs, were under the control of local education authorities and were intended to broaden the intake into higher education, and were competing in terms of image, reputation and facilities with universities of long standing which occupied a traditionally accepted position in the society of the day.

When we look at figures for 2021, however, the divide between pre-1992 and post-1992 does not seem to have changed much statistically but the explanation for the difference may be different at least as represented by the twelve institutions in this study. Rather than being determined by the level of the 'A' level scores demanded by the pre-1992 universities, as Whitburn et al. suggest that some 50 per cent of the intake in the mid-1970s were, the differences may now lie to a greater extent in the different missions that universities have adopted and the different conditions, financial and social, which may determine student choice.

For our analysis we have rejected artificial measures to determine regions such as distances in miles between the domicile of the student and the location of the university or local authority boundaries (unless these are used by the university) but have based our definition of region on whatever the universities themselves regarded as their region. This was not necessarily a student catchment area, though it sometimes was, but could be determined by geography, population density or the distribution of industry or public sector organizations. The intention is not to produce comparative rankings either of regional recruitment level or of graduate employment in domiciliary regions but to illustrate the different student-related relationships between institutions and their regions.

The pre- and post-1992 divide

Universities founded before 1992

The four pre-1992 universities we selected for illustrative purposes, Leeds, Newcastle, Lancaster and Stirling, comprise two urban-based Russell Group civic universities and two campus-based universities founded in the 1960s, one of which, Stirling, is located in Scotland. Leeds defines its region, tellingly, as 'the Leeds city region' with the same boundaries as the West Yorkshire Combined Authority covering Leeds City itself and Barnsley, Bradford, Calderdale, Craven, Harrogate, Kirklees, Leeds, Selby and Wakefield, an industrial region, socially mixed, covering areas of affluence and deprivation and considerable ethnic diversity; the LEP covers the same regional area thus ensuring a close partnership with the University in regeneration projects. Leeds is a large university with some 33,000 students including international students and postgraduates, and is in a region with a population of 3.2 million, roughly the size of Wales, yet only 14 per cent of its home undergraduate intake comes from its region and only 6 per cent from the city itself.

Newcastle defines its region more broadly as the North East covering a wide area between the Scottish border and Middlesbrough to the south and including both the North of Tyne Combined Authority and the North East Combined Authority (though the latter does not have a metro mayor) and covering the underpopulated Northumbria and the densely populated Tyneside. Along with Wales, the North East comprises one of the two least economically competitive regions in the country and has low higher education participation rates. The University has a long-established role in working with its community regarding its two key partners as the Newcastle City Council and the Newcastle Hospitals Foundation Trust but also maintains close links with some 100 schools in the area, and organizes summer schools to familiarize sixth-formers with university life. Nevertheless, around 76 per cent of its home undergraduate students come from outside the North East. Commenting on UCAS data on the average participation in higher education by eighteen-year-olds in 2020–1 a senior university figure pointed out that while London's participation rate was at over 56 per cent, the Newcastle region was firmly the 'at the bottom of the pile at 34 per cent' and that this was a

> 'very, very, very clear indicator ... that kids in the North East are less likely to go to university than anywhere else in the country and that has to reflect what we know about the levels of education, the levels of social deprivation up here.' (1)

Whereas Leeds and Newcastle Universities have grown up in major cities and in Leeds the University sits in a strongly industrial environment, Lancaster and Stirling were founded in semi-rural areas where the population was low and where there was little major industry. In both cases they lacked a clearly defined region. Lancaster could define its region as Lancashire and Cumbria, but the Cumberland half of Cumbria looks north towards Carlisle and Newcastle and the University's largest percentage of 'regional' undergraduate applications originates from the northern suburbs of Manchester; it, therefore, compromises by describing its region as the North West. Stirling, similarly, could adopt the Forth Valley, which includes Falkirk and Clackmannanshire, as its local region but prefers to identify its role towards a wider range of constituencies with the more generic description of the 'central belt of Scotland' which extends as far as Edinburgh, Glasgow and even up to Perth. Both universities have in their regions, areas of considerable economic disadvantage, Lancaster in Blackburn, Blackpool and the Fylde, and Stirling, in Clackmannanshire, one of the most deprived areas in the United Kingdom ranked 302 out of 376 in the 2019 UK Competitiveness Index. However, these universities, like Leeds and Newcastle, take only a minority of their UK undergraduate student numbers from their regions: Lancaster takes 45 per cent from the North West region as a whole but if you discount numbers coming from Manchester, Liverpool and Yorkshire the comparative figure is 27 per cent with Stirling standing at 24 per cent, and in this they share the character of almost all the pre-1992 universities. This is not at all to say that local or regional recruitment is not important to pre-1992 universities but that their history and student market position push them towards national rather than local recruitment strategies.

Universities created in 1992 and after

The nearest comparisons to the pre-1992 inner city-located universities Leeds and Newcastle described above, are Birmingham City University and the University of East London, both former polytechnics and both inner city-based institutions. For Birmingham City University the city is itself its region. As its 2025 Strategy document states:

> The majority of our students are from Birmingham and the broader West Midlands. They are the future of our city: its engineers and its health care professionals, its accountants and its lawyers, its teachers and its artists. We are Birmingham to the core. (Birmingham City University, *Strategy 2025*).

By comparison with Leeds, the University draws 58 per cent of its home students from the city in contrast to Leeds' 6 per cent and 71 per cent from the wider West Midlands against Leeds' 14 per cent from its region: it is primarily a local university, focusing its strategy on local employment needs and responding to local markets. Leeds would also see itself as a local university but would prioritize its contribution very differently.

The University of East London is in a different position to Birmingham City since it is located in a part of London, a very large capital city. The University relates most closely to its five local boroughs, Newham, where the University's three campuses are located, Barking and Dagenham, Tower Hamlets, Hackney, and Redbridge, which include some of the most deprived communities in the UK. It is also located within the Royal Docks Enterprise Zone, London's only LEP. Forty-one per cent of its students come from the five local boroughs and 80 per cent from London itself. What identifies it even more with its community is that 74 per cent are BAME students and that a high proportion are over the age of twenty-five. As with Birmingham City University, the great majority of these students do not look for accommodation provided by the university but travel daily from home, thus again emphasizing the 'neighbourhood' university role from the pre-1992 model. Both could be described as 'commuter' universities.

One other characteristic which reflects their particular inner-city location is that both universities have significant international student bodies. This international population is not so much a reflection of international prestige but arises from the presence of large immigrant communities which provide homes, and ultimately support, for relatives and friends from back home who wish to obtain a degree from an overseas university. This provides a resilient market for international students from certain countries which simply does not exist for many other much better known and more internationally prestigious institutions.

Two other former polytechnics, the Universities of Plymouth and South Wales offer further perspectives on how regions have framed their recruitment strategies. Plymouth is in effect the 'go to' university if you live in the South West and particularly on the peninsula and want to study from or within reach of home: 66 per cent of its home undergraduates come from the South West, 35 per cent from Devon alone. Moreover, across its twelve further education college partners, it has 3,220 students studying for a Plymouth award of which 1,200 are in science, 1,550 in arts and business, and 470 in health; across its extended region 4,000 students are studying nursing or health sciences. No university in England better illustrates the comparison of the mission of a 'neighbourhood' university with that of a Russell Group university (and Plymouth is also establishing a significant research reputation). The University of South Wales has an even more diverse region within which to operate and the economic state of the Cardiff Capital Region is more mixed than in the peninsula. As one member of the University described it:

> 'The Cardiff Capital Region is effectively south-east Wales; it's the ten local authorities there are in Cardiff and the surrounding area: Bridgend, Vale of Glamorgan, Rhondda Cynon Taf, Merthyr Tydfil, Caerphilly, Monmouthshire, Blaenau Gwent, Torfaen, Newport and Cardiff. It's Cardiff's equivalent of Greater Manchester if that makes sense ... It is a region of about 1.5 million people, so probably not far off half of the Welsh population.' (2)

Moreover, as a region it does not have the coherence which is apparent in the South West. Here, though, 76 per cent of its students come from the region with 36 per cent coming through the further education system. With this concentration it is not surprising that the University expresses its priorities as 'our core mission is absolutely our region ... we're unequivocal about this, we are rooted in our communities' (3). It is not difficult to see that the success of the University in reaching out to its community is of critical importance to a region which contains some of the most deprived areas in the UK.

The universities of Chester and Gloucestershire, both post-post-1992 universities, offer contrasting approaches to locality and region. Chester, like South Wales, is a widely distributed university in a very diverse area and operates regionally through a range of university centres. In Shrewsbury, working closely with the Shropshire Council, it has introduced courses in social work, nursing, teacher training, policing, and business studies, and is planning to build up its numbers there from 500 to 750 within two years. In Warrington, where a downtown campus is being established, numbers are at 1,200 and are planned to double in the near future. Additionally, it has a sixty-acre science park, Thornton Science Park, next to the Stanlow Oil Refinery which is focused on renewable energy and the energy sector, on which it intends to develop teaching facilities. Overall, 60 per cent of its home intake comes from its region.

The Chester story is very different to Gloucestershire's, though they had very similar institutional origins, simply because of the locations and the way they have addressed them – Chester within close to Liverpool and Manchester Universities both with well-established Russell Group reputations, and Gloucestershire hedged around, though at greater distance, by Bristol, Birmingham and Oxford. Chester has followed the more adventurous route of spreading its wings into a diverse area some of whose characteristics and needs have produced a profile very much at variance with that of its predecessor college of higher education. Gloucestershire, on the other hand, has followed the more local path of knitting together its two campuses in Cheltenham and Gloucester and concentrating, with support from the county and from the LEP, on working to meet the needs of the narrower base of the single county of Gloucestershire: 'the economic effect is that we're creating the skilled labour force of the future for the county' (4). Like Chester, however, a majority of its home students are local – 56 per cent live within fifty-five miles of one of the two campuses.

We conclude this section with two universities whose models are different again from post-1992 and post-post-1992 models. The first is Lincoln. Embracing a very large region, on a north-south axis from the Humber to the Wash and with the fringes of the East Midlands to the west and the North Sea to the east, the region as a whole ranks low on all the economic indicators with its commercial base dominated, as in the south west, by SMEs, often very small family businesses. But Lincoln, untrammelled by regional university competition except perhaps from Nottingham University which is a significantly southward facing institution in terms of student recruitment, has set itself the ambitious task of using its presence and its academic skills explicitly in the cause of regional regeneration. The region, as one senior officer told us, is one that 'classically, in UK terms, needs levelling up' (5). As one aspect of this, 76 per cent of the University's intake comes from the region – one wonders how many of this intake would even have sought university entrance if the University had not existed? The figures break down by sub region as 25.9 per cent from Lincolnshire, 15.2 per cent from Yorkshire and Humberside, 13 per cent from the East Midlands and 12 per cent from the East of England reflecting the character of the region and the gap in higher education opportunities which the University is seeking to fill. The second university is the Highlands and Islands University in Scotland. This offers a radically different model of a university to anything else in the UK and, uniquely, was created to meet a particular regional need. Initially planned with the prime objective of providing a way of counteracting migration out of the region, it has developed into a widely distributed university which recruits its students through thirteen institutional partner routes. In total 67 per cent of its home undergraduate intake comes from within the region but the proportions differ considerably between the component institutions so that, for example, 91 per cent of the entrants from the Shetlands are from the region and 84 per cent and 83 per cent respectively of the nursing departments in Inverness and Stornoway are recruited locally. The Highlands and Islands University represents the most extreme form of the regional university in the UK and its structure is not likely to be replicated if only because its region has characteristics not found elsewhere except possibly in the south west. As Scotland moves towards a tertiary higher education system the Highlands and Islands model may become increasingly less unusual within Scotland.

A summary of the figures is provided in Table 3.1.

Closing the pre- and post-1992 divide

What the foregoing demonstrates is the sharply differing patterns of local student recruitment employed within the twelve institutions ranging from 14 per cent in Leeds to 76 per cent in Lincoln. It has also shown that the 1960s New Universities, while radical in their approach to academic disciplines,

Table 3.1 Proportion of each university's home students recruited from the University's region (2017–18)

University	%
Leeds	14
Newcastle	24
Lancaster	27 (45 from the broader North West)
Stirling	24
Birmingham City	58 (71 from the West Midlands)
East London	36 from the five boroughs (78 from London)
Plymouth	66
South Wales	76
Gloucestershire	56 (from within 55 miles of the University)
Chester	79
Lincoln	76
Highlands and Islands	67

modelled themselves, consciously or unconsciously, on their civic predecessors in seeing their primary response as being to a national rather than a local or regional student market. Post-1992 universities have tackled local markets energetically and worked hard to create new ones. Partly this was out of self-interest when pre-1992 universities were attracting the most and the best qualified candidates but increasingly they are responding to a changed set of priorities where social criteria now play a much larger role in the process of applying to a university. Financial pressures alone are making local universities more attractive to many families while the impact of Covid-19 may have increased discouragement to study too far away from home.

However, the extent to which the post-1992 universities suffered reputationally because of when they were established and the fact that their extended period as polytechnics positioned them as a second tier of the then higher education ranking system, can perhaps be put into historical perspective by studying the history of the civic universities of an earlier period. Thus, in 1938 Leeds took 90 per cent of its total numbers (including international students) from Yorkshire, 66 per cent coming from the West Riding alone. By 1954, the Yorkshire figure had fallen to 46.4 per cent and by 1964 to 28 per cent with 58 per cent coming from the rest of England (University of Leeds Archive, *Senate Agenda* No. 13 1964). In 1938, and even in 1954, the figures give it a student recruitment profile remarkably like that of Birmingham City University today.

By good fortune we also have a description of the University as it was in 1936 by one of its graduates, Richard Hoggart, (later Assistant Secretary General of UNESCO, Principal of Goldsmiths College, University of London, and, most famously, author of *The Uses of Literacy*, 1957), Hoggart, as a day student travelling daily by urban transport from Hunslet to the University, attended a university of 1,700 students, of whom 1,300 'came from nearby' (76 per cent) and 324 from the city itself. He describes his intake as forming three groups of students: the wealthy middle class, sons of West Riding mill owners; a middle group of 'the less well to do' and a third 'the really local and the poorest, lower middle class and some working class and most in the Arts subjects ... [who] came to the University each day on the tram from parts of Leeds itself or from as far afield as Bradford all of nine miles away' (Hoggart 1988: 185). The origin of its students gave it a local and regional character:

the fact that many of the Leeds students went back each night to the streets of the city or the townships around, or slipped at weekends to their homes in the Ridings, ensured that the University was felt to be part of the area in a way not easy to bring about today; its affairs and events were talked about in homes all around and became part of the folklore and fabric of day-by-day life. (Hoggart 1988: 187)

When we think of the massive, high reputation university that Leeds has become over eighty years or so, we need to ask ourselves where Birmingham City, East London, Lincoln or Plymouth Universities might be over the same period. The development of Leeds was primarily driven by the expansion of student numbers after the 1963 Robbins Report but it was also a consequence of its dominant location in the city and the city's own development to becoming a prosperous provincial capital. Similar social, economic and political change may also affect the reputational and academic standing of many of the post-1992 universities.

Graduate outcomes: the regional impact

Mapping the percentage input of a region into a university's student intake tells us a great deal about the university's integration with its region and the reputation it has within its community. It also, of course, reflects the impact of competition within a diverse higher education sector where universities are by no means competing on a level playing field. The current shape of higher education encourages a league-table mentality the results of which may have very little relevance to relationships to regions. Nationally there are many high profile universities, like Leeds and Newcastle in this study, which are making a remarkable impact in transforming city centres by building innovation hubs or engaging in similar ventures which will create the climate to bring international companies and high-level employment to the region. A statement in the brochure for the Newcastle Helix, a twenty-four-acre development in the Newcastle city centre, sums up the key elements of the approach:

Newcastle Helix is a unique partnership between Newcastle City Council, Newcastle University and Legal and General. Our vision is to create a destination that attracts global talent, harnesses the intellectual horsepower from the University, and taps into the drive from the Council to create economic growth in the city and lasting change. (Newcastle City Council et al. 2020)

However, this does not tell the whole story. It takes no account of the University's most important product, its students, and the impact they will make economically, socially and in civic engagement to the future of society and the economy. A current measure of university success is graduate salary levels, but this inevitably favours job seeking in areas of high employment and may have the perverse effect of creating incentives which discourage graduates from returning to their domiciliary regions. (Kollydas and Green show that 32.3 of all home UK students graduating in 2018–19 were employed after fifteen months in London (WMREDI/C-REDI 2022). To use salary post-graduation as any kind of policy pointer could, in the words of Donnelly and Gamsu (Donnelly and Gamsu 2018: 25), 'act to entrench regional divisions by drawing able students away from deprived marginalised areas'. We need to remember that the *raison d'être* of the Highlands and Islands University, was not initially to widen participation, although it has done this, but to reverse the trend for students in the north of Scotland to go south for their higher education, never to return. The success of the policy can be seen in the statistics quoted in Table 3.2 below. A parallel economic motive for resisting the 'up and away' role of higher education was voiced by the Leader of Peterborough City Council when he launched his Authority's bid for a university in 2020 saying 'it is the biggest thing we can do to stop talented young people from leaving Peterborough and to give our businesses a good crop of people to apply for jobs' (ARU Peterborough, 14 July 2020). The importance of the reintegration of graduates into their home communities has not been sufficiently recognized or encouraged.

We should not exaggerate the impact of transforming city centres with innovation hubs. They may greatly enhance the commercial reputation of a city, carry prestige, provide space and facilities for new companies, and thus provide increased employment opportunities but they may only have a transient effect and the employment opportunities may not extend very far down the qualifications ladder. High profile investments in inner cities also run the risk of sucking out the best qualified members of just these pockets of impoverishment and deprivation that current policies find it so hard to penetrate. Universities' educational role as potentially offering an alternative and more sustained contribution to human capital needs greater emphasis. If we want to see a long-term 'levelling up' we need to give at least equal weight to encouraging graduates to return to their communities not to leave them after graduation for better prospects elsewhere. In a situation where 43.7 per cent of working people never leave the area where they were born one solution to the regeneration of these communities is not to weaken them further but to encourage their reinforcement by re-absorbing their most enterprising products back into that environment.

Schuller et al.'s *The Benefits of Learning* (2004) provides clear evidence that 'learning, further education, provides key attributes which can enable the individual or the community to grow and develop' (Schuller et al. 2004: 29). It suggests that education in such communities can offer the following:

- human capital – 'the knowledge and skills possessed by individuals which enable them to function effectively in economic and social life' (Schuller et al. 2004: 14)
- social capital – the networks and norms which enable people to contribute to common goals, for example civic activities
- identity capital – 'education has a leading role in people's understanding of and confidence in their own identity' (Schuller et al. 2004: 19).

Willetts provides an excellent summary of the identifiable wider benefits to be obtained in general by all those gaining a university education (Willetts 2017: 139–41) but Schuller et al. focus particularly on the benefits to be obtained by members of disadvantaged or 'left behind' communities from opportunities to re-engage with education perhaps initially on a part time basis. They conclude:

> Huge costs are incurred when learning is absent. Poor physical and psychological health, malfunctioning families and communities lacking in social glue: all these are partial consequences of inadequate education. (Schuller et al. 2004: 192)

As one vice-chancellor of a post-1992 university, who had had experience of working in a Russell Group and other post-1992 institutions, testified:

> 'I can say, hand on heart, that our graduates ... are some of the most talented and resilient and entrepreneurial and innovative students that I've met in my

twenty-five years [in universities] but they may not have the full suite of scaffolding, kind of social capital, that enables them to put some of that expertise into practice in a typically kind of more traditional, let's call it middle class, white male professional practice. And so part of our job of work is to equip our students with that necessary social capital.' (6)

Universities, working as individual institutions or in collaboration with further education college partners, offer key sources of encouragement to such communities to realize the many talents they possess. In a period when the fashion to pursue higher education at a distance from home appears to be in decline and commuting from home, or at least enrolling in a local institution, is achieving greater acceptance, some universities are active in closing the gaps with deprived communities as a way of easing the return of the graduates to the community from which they came. There are many reasons why staying local may be attractive – family considerations, financial or cultural and social – so that even entertaining the idea of entering higher education without the availability of easy unpressured access may be ruled out. Having entered, however, it is important that the only recognized concept of success, moving to employment 'hot spots' elsewhere, should be dispelled; returning to regenerate one's own community should be regarded as being of equal value. Deprived communities will not be regenerated by innovation hubs in major cities, though they may have their place in a levelling-up programme, but by civic leadership, by the recruitment of new graduates into family-based SMEs or to the health-related services and by a regular flow of new teachers into the school system. Certainly, these communities need capital investment but for a longer-term reduction of inequalities an investment in human capital is required; returning graduates represent a key component offering the prospect of providing 'high quality jobs' to their communities thus contributing to a local economy driven by 'agglomeration and spill overs' (Feldman 2000). These communities may need to be helped, however, to help themselves.

These conclusions are reinforced by a study undertaken by the Bridge Group for the UPP Foundation (Bridge Group 2021). This was a small-scale study of four universities, two pre-1992 and two post-1992 (but no post-post-1992) together with interviews with thirty-five graduates but the directions of its findings underline some of the themes of our own research. It confirms the picture of the difference between pre- and post-1992 universities in the proportion of graduates who have local backgrounds staying on to seek employment in their home areas. Such graduates it finds are likely to be from lower socio-economic backgrounds, are more likely to represent the first generation of their family to go to university and more likely to have been mature students aged twenty-five or above. It concludes that:

> Our interviews with graduates showed that decisions to stay local after graduating were guided by considerations of well-being, financial independence and health. Graduates who stayed on were pursuing social mobility through using their social networks to land graduate jobs and capitalizing on lower living costs to save towards investing in property – a source of financial security in later life (Bridge Group 2021: 5, para 9).

In other words, the perception of a higher education market promoting competition to enter the most selective universities does not resonate with a substantial tranche of potential university applicants who are driven by different kinds of domestic, economic and social aspirations. This represents a significant re-balancing of priorities from a widespread view that higher education institutions serve an important 'up and away' function encouraging graduates to move to high value locations which provide higher salaries and apparently more stimulating life styles to a recognition of the virtues of regional as opposed to metropolitan living. (An IFS study shows that around half of Oxbridge graduates live in London by age twenty-seven while the proportion is less than 10 per cent for the least selective universities (Britton et al. 2021).) Without universities or further education colleges in their locality many applicants would probably not seek to enter higher education at all and the character of their graduate contribution to their community would be lost.

It is important, therefore, to see the extent to which a university's graduates return to their regions as a crucial element in an institution's relationship with its region. Rather than rely on national data collections we have chosen, as with defining the regions, to seek data direct from universities on the proportionate 'deposit' of their graduates in their regions. Because the regions are so variable in size no attempt has been made to rank these percentages and the figures for each university are therefore listed below in the order in which, as described above, they recruited students from their region into the university.

Table 3.2 Proportion of each university's home undergraduates opting to work in the region in which they undertook their studies (2017–18)

University	%
Leeds	33.7
Newcastle	34.6
Lancaster	31.5 (but for Cumbria and Lancashire alone 13.4%)
Stirling	24
Birmingham City	71 (69 for Birmingham City alone)
East London	59 (12 for the 5 boroughs)*
Plymouth	63
South Wales	*Data not available*
Gloucestershire	31
Chester	54.7
Lincoln	71.3
Highlands and Islands	76 (but 95% for returners overall)

* Figures for employment only and therefore not comparable with data from other universities

These figures emphasize the regional impact of university graduate populations. It is noticeable that in the cases of Leeds and Newcastle the proportion of their graduates staying on in the universities' region considerably exceeds the proportion of the intake who come from the region, 14 per cent and 24 per cent respectively. In both cases this reflects the attractiveness of the city and the region to their 'in comer' graduates but is reinforced by the existence in each university of a large medical school that produces a significant graduate 'deposit'. Leeds has, of course, the advantage for graduate employment of also being a heavily industrialized city with strengths in the financial and legal support services. On the other hand, the two campus universities, Lancaster and Stirling, located on the periphery of much smaller urban centres, have much lower staying on figures reflecting the different economic context in which they are located. In both cases they operate primarily as bases from which graduates look outwards for their future employment.

Birmingham City University offers a direct contrast; not only do 71 per cent take employment in the region, 69 per cent within the Birmingham Local Authority area itself, but almost 50 per cent of the total have come out of the lowest multiple deprivation quintile and 54 per cent are BAME. East London's figures are 59 per cent and 74 per cent of their students are BAME. Plymouth University follows a similar pattern with 63 per cent entering the University from its south-west region and 63 per cent returning to it, 33.3 per cent to Devon itself. In many ways, the most surprising sets of figures come from the universities founded since 2000. Gloucestershire and Chester have broken free of their previous concentration on teacher training to engage with much wider social areas of recruitment while Lincoln and the Highlands and Islands have accomplished an exceptional impact on their regions essentially from a standing start. Lincoln has demonstrated an extraordinary ability to engage with its region with over 70 per cent of its graduates, 30 per cent in Lincolnshire itself, having returned to take employment in a region previously starved of a higher education institution. The figures for the Highlands and Islands triumphantly confirm the ideas of its founders by showing that 95 per cent of its registered students stay in its area, 76 per cent in employment, and do not migrate from the region to the south. Both institutions are engaged in transformative processes within their regions; equally, both are mission-driven by their regions in ways that are distinctive amongst comparator universities.

What this chapter demonstrates are the different impacts different kinds of universities can make on the human capital of their localities and regions. If we look at Leeds University through the eyes of Richard Hoggart in the late 1930s, we are looking at a university which was essentially local in its student body and served primarily its surrounding region, a position that was paralleled in all the provincial civic universities of that period. Over time that mission has changed but both Leeds and Newcastle have become instead net importers of qualified graduates into their regions. These regions are also more economically structured to offer employment than those in which Lancaster and Stirling are located.

The universities founded later, in the post-1992 era, are all much more regional universities because their catchment remains primarily local. They have not had the benefits of the long build-up of research investment which, along with the immediate post-Robbins expansion, transformed the civic universities to produce a national market. But it could be argued that the universities founded after 1992 have, in effect, replaced Leeds and the other older civic universities of the 1930s in addressing their local markets, but have also taken the local and regional mission much more proactively into their communities than their predecessor institutions ever felt the need to do. Their role has become not simply complementary to those of earlier generations but offers an altogether broader set of institutional solutions to attacking the problems of regional inequality.

Chapter 4

The Intersectoral Interface: Universities and Further Education

Relationships between further and higher education

Historically the development of the university system proceeded quite separately from the growth of further education. The autonomy of the university system was protected by the University Grants Committee (UGC), but further education was in the hands of the local education authorities which were free to develop their colleges in the way they thought best suited to their circumstances. In 1967 the then secretary of state, Tony Crosland, in a speech given at Woolwich Technical College (now the University of Greenwich), announced the creation of a polytechnic system, to be created out of the further education colleges. The thirty polytechnics were to remain under local authority control occupying city locations, but one effect was to lower the standing of the colleges not selected for upgrading to polytechnic status and to turn them into a third tier of post-secondary education. In 1988, the polytechnics, which had outgrown their local education authority controls, were transferred to a new central authority, the Polytechnics and Colleges Funding Council. Four years later they were given university status and the further education colleges were also removed from local authority control and given legal independence but which otherwise left their educational status unchanged.

The 1992 Act decentralized the control of higher education to separate funding councils in England, Scotland and Wales (Northern Ireland already had separate powers). Further education was also decentralized and in England was put under a Further Education Funding Council. Thirty years later, Wales has removed the division between further and higher education and has opted for a tertiary education system more appropriate to its economic and geophysical circumstances; Scotland, where historically 20 per cent of higher education is carried out within further education, seems to be following suit. In England, however, funding for the sector and control remains centralized through an Education and Skills Funding Agency (ESFA) located under the Department for Education (DfE).

The decision to move further education from the control of the local education authorities in 1992 was partly a reflection of the government's lack of confidence in the local authorities and partly to introduce the discipline of the market into the sector by making funding dependent on student recruitment. In England, the result was a consolidation in the numbers of institutions prompted by widespread mergers. Thus, the total of 465 colleges that were removed from local authority control in 1992 (Smithers and Robinson 2000) fell to 435 by the year 2000 (Melville and Macleod 2000) and was reduced yet further to 294 by 2019 (with England at 248, Scotland at twenty-six, Wales fourteen and Northern Ireland six (Shattock and Hunt 2021). The reductions in the number of institutions did not necessarily affect the distribution of teaching locations because mergers generally preserved the merged college sites in order to facilitate access by students in the area. For example, in Coventry, where four colleges merged to form City College Coventry, the sites of all four colleges remain teaching hubs for the institution. The important point which this reflects is that although the number of colleges has fallen, the distributed nature of most colleges has preserved their ability to reach out into their local communities for students, a process which has been encouraged by the open-ended funding mechanisms adopted by the Funding Agency.

Although the two sectors have remained administratively separate (until recently in Wales), collaboration between institutions across the sectoral line has been growing and has significantly re-shaped the activities of some universities. Market drivers in terms of student recruitment in both universities and colleges have encouraged the process: in some universities, recruitment pressures have required national recruitment to be strongly supplemented from local markets; in colleges, the availability of the possibility of progression towards higher education qualifications without changing institutions represents a prestige factor in recruitment. In addition, it offers colleges the prospect of income supplementation through the recruitment of higher education students paying higher education tuition fees. But increasingly in both sectors, activities are also driven by perceptions of inequality, the need to widen participation, and the social and economic arguments for greater community involvement. Recognition of the public good is becoming more important than market motivations. A senior officer at the University of Plymouth summed up the underlying importance of university/college collaboration in the following statement:

> 'there's very much a culture within our partner network and we meet regularly as a group, we have a partner forum three times a year, where all of them [college representatives] come together with us and it's about sharing good practice, that's what it's always been about. And in that is a very strong culture that what we are trying to achieve is providing higher education opportunities and you don't ever need to stop.... I've seen ... how transformative higher education can be for people's lives, it is a good thing, it's fundamentally a good thing that I do ... for an individual student, the best progression opportunity is whatever the best progression opportunity is, and that may be to get out of Cornwall and go somewhere else and have a better, a broader [life], expand your horizons, that sort of thing. And for other students ... the best opportunity is actually at your local university, and where there's a range of opportunity as well.' (1)

What we have been able to uncover in a separate survey (Shattock and Hunt 2021) is that of a 45 per cent response rate from UK colleges, 89 per cent indicated that they had joint arrangements or direct partnerships with at least one university and that ninety-five universities, over half the number of UK universities, were involved. The activities covered in the survey were student progression, franchising arrangements, validation agreements and agreements to extend apprenticeship programmes into degree work. Of these, student progression and validation agreements were by far the most common.

The college/university interface

It is not surprising that links between post-1992 universities and colleges are considerably more extensive than those of pre-1992 universities: of 369 formal links between universities and colleges recorded in the Shattock and Hunt survey, 49 per cent involved post-1992 universities and 25 per cent post-post-1992 universities as compared with only 5 per cent for Russell Group universities and 21 per cent for non-Russell Group pre-1992 universities. (The figure for the post-post-1992 universities may be a reflection of the number of universities in the group and their disciplinary spread.) There may be several explanations for the figures:

- In a competitive recruitment market pre-1992 universities have historically been less likely to need relationships with further education colleges to meet their admission targets.
- Applicants to university via further education colleges are more likely to be older, to be locally based and intending to live at home or locally and to apply later in the UCAS cycle than applicants to pre-1992 universities.
- The post-1992 universities, when they were polytechnics, had much closer relationships with further education colleges than the pre-1992 universities.

This differential engagement with further education reflects the historical positions of the universities founded before and after 1992 and the way that they traditionally address the recruitment of students. As one interviewee from a post 1992 university expressed it, his university:

> 'both as a polytechnic and now, has put priority on helping students with disadvantaged backgrounds to find pathways through education into the world of employment. In the past much of the commitment was towards the delivery of sub-degree qualifications like the Higher National Certificate of the Higher National Diploma as a stage towards obtaining a degree. Now the object is to offer opportunities [to obtain full degrees] for those kind of students [for whom] school didn't work out but they've still got the ability and the aptitude to succeed at a higher level ... so it's a second chance kind of market to help people progress and become established in their careers. ... The kind of stuff the league tables are interested in doesn't tell the full story for universities like ours because they're into that traditional ... gone for 'A' levels, done a three-year degree, come out the other end of the sausage machine straight into a blue chip [job] ... Well we're different to that, you know, we are offering something of a different shape.' (2)

A feature of these university partnerships with colleges is the way it both extends the opportunity to obtain higher education into the local community and extends its source away from a single institutional site thus creating a very different structural form from that of the older university model. As one university told us:

> 'We do get a pipeline of students coming directly on to first degrees and studying at the university. Now, we've also got a relationship with a number of FE partner colleges where those students never set foot in [the university] physically and they'll do the whole of their study at another location ... [In some franchised] programmes they'll do the first two years in the FE college and then they'll come to the university for the final year ... but there are a number of courses that are delivered entirely at those FE partners.' (3)

It is worth adding that another attraction for university relationships with further education is that the latter appear to be more successful than schools in widening participation: according to the Sutton Trust when further education colleges are compared to sixth form schools and colleges facing similar challenges young people with disadvantaged backgrounds are more likely to achieve entry to higher education from further education colleges (Lisauskaite et al. 2021).

University/college network structures

Four examples from our case study institutions, Plymouth, Lincoln, Chester and South Wales, illustrate the extent of the network structures being created. In each case, these universities are addressing large regions, all of them notable for low participation and high levels of economic and social deprivation. Plymouth has established a twelve-college network (Bridgewater and Taunton, City of Bristol, City College Plymouth, Cornwall College Group, Exeter, Highlands College Jersey, Petroc, Strode, South Devon, Truro and Penwith, Weymouth, and Yeovil) extending from the six Cornish college sites in the Cornish Group up as far as Bristol; the Cornish College Group in the far south west of the peninsula has over 800 students registered for Plymouth programmes, and the South Devon College much closer to Plymouth, over 600. At Lincoln, the University has partnerships with six colleges, the Grimsby Institute, North Lindsey, Bishop Burton, Boston, Grantham, and Lincoln colleges which are linked to the University through an Institute of Technology created out of funding from the Government and supported by the LEP. Chester has partnership arrangements with the following colleges: Cheshire College East and West, Macclesfield, Reaseheath, Warrington and Vale and Wirral Metropolitan College, the last spread over four campuses in the Wirral. The University of South Wales has five further education college partnerships, Bridgend, Cardiff and Vale, which covers the Vale of Glamorgan, Coleg Gwent, Cymraeg, which is the college of the Valleys (and covers most of the Valleys not covered by Bridgend and Merthyr Tydfil), and Merthyr Tydfil College.

Merthyr Tydfil College, however, is different: in 2006 it was taken over by the University of Glamorgan and became a constituent college of the University of South Wales when that institution was created by the merger of the University of Glamorgan and the University of Wales, Newport in 2013. The College continues to have its own governing body on which the University is fully represented, but operates in close alignment with the University, acting in a unique way as a bridge between the University and the community. In 2010, the Merthyr Tydfil local education authority transferred sixth-form teaching in schools in the town to the college so that it is possible to enter the college at age sixteen and continue on into higher education, through the agency of the University, without students leaving their home town. Merthyr Tydfil is one of the most deprived towns not just in Wales but in the UK. As a senior member of staff told us:

> 'our learners are very lucky that they have a university on their doorstep; they can obviously study with us at the college, or they can go onto the parent company [that is, the University]. Without that opportunity to study locally I fear that not many of them would even consider higher education as an option.... there is still, all these years on from the introduction of fees and HE fees, that huge stigma about debt so you know having that opportunity to study locally makes a huge difference to them because without it they would not go.' (4)

The College provides a striking example of how the interlinking of a university and a college can enable higher education to reach deeply into local communities. In Merthyr Tydfil a senior member of the College told us:

> 'whilst we recruit 89 per cent of learners from local schools there are a core of learners in local schools many of whom will not do GCSEs.... Many of

them have got very low skill levels, they are disengaged from education, many of them have been referred through to pupil referral units because of behaviour issues and they are very hard to reach and to get them to engage in vocational learning which may be more appropriate than the curriculum they may have encountered in schools.' (5)

They thus fall into the category of NEETs (Not in Education, Employment or Training). The College in close collaboration with the schools, has devised a new curriculum, constructed at a lower level than normal Level 3 entry based on prior attainment, usual in further education, and uses literacy and numeracy tests to admit students. The College has reduced the drop-out rate in the first eight weeks to 4 per cent and, for those who go on to GCSE/'A' levels, only 1 per cent, but the rate is highest among adult entrants who have been out of education for some years: 'it's that realization of trying to juggle work, family life and study for many of them they find particularly difficult' (6). Students from Merthyr Tydfil and the Valleys, former coal-mining areas, are singularly reluctant to move out of their area and away from an inward-looking culture. Students successfully completing the two-year Foundation Degree at the college were unwilling to pursue the third top-up year for the full university degree at the University's Treforest campus in Pontypridd no more than ten miles away – 'they liked the fact that they could study locally and when I say local, I mean in their town' (7) – so the University took the decision to transfer the teaching from the University down to the college. The college thus plays a critical role in nurturing access to educational qualifications whether at 'A' level, vocational or higher education levels working with students from one of the most impoverished locations in the UK. From a university perspective about 450 students, including part-times, leave the college each year for higher education, about 60 per cent of them going to the University of South Wales.

A further, and from a public service point of view, extremely valuable contribution from the university/college linkage, is in nursing. The Prince Charles Hospital is the largest employer in Merthyr Tydfil and the University provision of nursing education plays a critical role both in the services which the hospital can provide and in the general field of widening participation. The proximity of the hospital and the university/college partnership offers a route to an attractive career for young people, particularly girls from the Valleys. They can become 'bank' nurses, that is join the NHS bank of casual nursing staff, then enter the college's health and welfare programme as a preliminary to entering the University's nursing degree, undertaking their practice periods in the local hospital. On graduation they can hope to take up permanent employment in the Hospital providing a culturally local service to local patients.

What this account of the interface between a college and a university illustrates is that it can enable universities to reach out even into a small town of about 60,000 people to provide an educational infrastructure which offers the prospect of change to one of the UK's most impoverished environments. Without the efforts of the College, without the availability of nursing as a career and without the University's strong sense of civic mission significant numbers of young people would simply not have had the opportunity to enable them to achieve the kinds of education and qualifications necessary to contribute to the modern economy or to obtain the social capital to enable them to give social and economic leadership within their own communities. Universities are not well structured on their own to interface with communities in this way, but further education colleges can be and the linkage of mission and purpose of the two categories of institution and the outreach provided by the colleges represent one of the most important approaches to reducing the inequalities so apparent within the UK. Undoubtedly, one of the underlying grounds for the particular developments in Merthyr Tydfil is the constitutional relationship between the University and the College. Although there are parallel constitutional arrangements elsewhere in the UK, they are rare except in Scotland where the University of the Highlands is based on a federation of colleges and research establishments operating under a corporate umbrella, with central offices in Inverness. The breadth of this university's remit goes far beyond the South Wales-Merthyr Tydfil concept because it covers an enormously wide and diverse geographical area. However, a visit to the Lews Castle College of Further Education Stornoway in the Outer Hebrides, with its 2,700 students presenting itself as a campus of a University of the Highlands and Islands some 100 miles, including a sea crossing, away is to encounter a remarkable vision of a university/college relationship reaching out to a remote community. The fact, as described in Chapter 3, that such a high proportion of the University's graduates remain in the area in which they studied makes it the ultimate example of the regional university.

The pre-1992 universities and the colleges

For the reasons described above most pre-1992 universities have engaged with further education colleges far less vigorously than the post- and the post-post-1992s. Historically this was not always the case: the University of London external degree arrangements with colleges of the nineteenth century can look remarkably like the validation arrangements entered into by universities and colleges in the modern period. Nevertheless, this is not to say that individual partnerships do not flourish amongst the pre-1992 partnerships although it is also evident that their nature depends to a considerable extent on the history and location of the different institutions. The civic universities in the Russell Group, for example, are not dependent on further education colleges for reaching recruitment targets, usually the first rationale for universities to enter college partnerships, because there is no immediate direct incentive to do so but a further inhibition is that with former polytechnics, now universities, often located adjoining them in inner city sites, they have no wish to appear to be entering into competition with neighbours with whom they have congenial collaborative relationships (Leeds Beckett University's boundaries abut Leeds University's, and Northumbria University's site is not much further away from Newcastle University's with Sunderland University's also only a mile away). However, change may be on its way, and it is perhaps significant that Newcastle has signed a memorandum of understanding for the creation of a strategic partnership with the Newcastle College Group from whom it takes a significant group of students each year. The establishment of funding streams for apprenticeship degrees offers a new prospect for collaboration for universities with strong engineering programmes.

The position of our two 1960s New Universities is different again. Coming, as we have described above, more recently, to a broader social and regional agenda both are now in active collaboration with colleges but their opportunities for impact are more limited by their locations. Lancaster is very anxious to be seen as relevant to its community, but it is in an area of low population which lacks a secure industrial base. Its main contribution is, therefore, to the Blackpool and Fylde peninsula some thirty-eight driving miles away from the University. This is a deeply impoverished area made up of coastal holiday towns and rural areas with the nearest access to universities being to Lancaster and Preston (the University of Central Lancashire). Lancaster has an extended partnership with Blackpool and The Fylde College, a large four-campus college which itself has awarding powers for the Foundation Degree. As of 2019–20, the College had over 2,000 students studying for Lancaster qualifications, the largest validation partnership in England, and is the prime access route to higher education in the area. However, Lancaster also retains what might be described as a pre-1992 approach seeing itself as 'an attracter of talent in, and if that talent comes in there is hope that some will stay, some will create businesses, some will make a home' (8) in effect accepting that in its geographical placement makes it more likely to be able to contribute to the local and regional economy by being an agent for importing qualified graduates than by measures aimed at widening participation through local recruitment.

Stirling University has the advantage of being the only university in the Forth Valley, a region which has only one further education college, the Forth Valley College with campuses in Stirling, Alloa and Falkirk. The University has two outstanding areas of collaboration with the College. The first is a partnership to deliver the innovation stream, which the University leads, in the Stirling and Clackmannanshire City Region Deal, a UK Government project planned to bring £48 million alone for innovation into the region. The second is a joint (or integrated) degree between the University, the College and employer groups where university students benefit from the practical training provided by the college and work placements made available by the employers. In both universities the arrangements thus demonstrate the value of the university/college partnership to the universities themselves, to the colleges and to the communities.

The management of the interface

The picture that can be drawn across the UK of the relations between further and higher education suggest a progressive integration of interests. In Wales and in Scotland, it is evident that this has gone a lot farther than in England. In Wales, there were twenty-six colleges in 1992, with the number now reduced by mergers to fourteen. This consolidation has not been achieved by state fiat but by persuasion and extended consultation. The creation of the university/college network together with the merger of the University of Glamorgan with University College Newport demonstrates how higher education can be reformed without recourse to heavy-handed arbitrary government intervention. The key is the fact of the close links and mutual understanding between the Welsh Department of Education and Skills and the senior officers of the colleges and universities. As one senior college officer told us:

> 'we're very sort of closely connected to the Welsh Government ... we've got a chief executive of an FE college in England on our board and he's amazed how much close dialogue we have directly with Welsh government officials – it's literally pick up the phone and speak to them, you drop them a personal email, whereas in England it's very much, you know, arm's length. So that does allow us to have that close discussion with the Welsh government so that they appreciate the challenges that FE colleges are facing in this current climate.' (9)

In England, a much greater reliance has been placed on market forces to determine the shape of the sector with the initiative being largely left to the colleges themselves based on their own institutional strategic self-interest. Since funding has been determined by student numbers, college strategies have been driven by the need to meet the student head count targets. This has led to very competitive markets being established especially where colleges are in reasonable proximity to one another. In many ways this policy has been successful: the close relationship between central government and the colleges in Wales, could not be replicated in such a large system as in England; the 1992 spectrum of colleges has been rationalized without overbearing state intervention and colleges and universities have come together of their own volition to form partnerships for their mutual benefit.

On the other hand, reliance on market forces alone does not create stability especially when both college and university sectors are highly marketized and are liable to take short-term decisions about new programmes or competitive relationships which may be in their institutions' interests but not in those of potential students where secure long-term strategies for course offerings are desirable. One important area of tension is in relation to tuition fees: colleges claiming higher education numbers can thereby supplement their further education income. As one vice-chancellor expressed it: 'they have to keep their organizations solvent as well so they are looking for opportunities to recruit and earn fee income and they'll go where they think they can earn fee income' (10). This can put universities and colleges into direct competition for students. Only a few colleges have exclusive relationships with universities. This is understandable because maintaining open relationships preserves a college's independence in negotiating collaboration agreements but is also good for students as it offers them wider ongoing opportunities than simply being committed to a single university. Moreover, a single university might not be able to produce matching subject expertise of the right depth for progression or validation purposes. Nevertheless, from a university perspective, coordinating a college network where colleges have a variety of institutional ambitions and where each partnership or joint activity arrangement has been negotiated and agreed separately, can be a politically demanding task and stability depends on trust between the institutions. As the vice-chancellor quoted above claimed: 'where we have a good strong partnership with local FE colleges it is very much based on understanding where can we collaborate and where can we compete' (11).

But if universities are concerned about changes in colleges' strategies, how much more so must colleges be at risk of changes in universities' priorities as a result of changes in academic personnel, institutional changes of direction or changes in government policy? And where is the student long-term interest protected or the interests of the economy and society in the pursuit of continuity of efforts to recruit students from low participation neighbourhoods which may require long-term financial support to prove to be economically viable? There is thus a balance of interests to be respected in a situation where the corporate and financial interests of the universities and the colleges are almost bound to dominate. There are very many advantages in protecting the long-term rights of colleges and universities to create partnerships entirely on their own initiative, but one improvement might be for a broadly common contract to be agreed that specifies standard terms for partnerships and defines their projected joint activities and their review periods for use by the participating institutions. Many universities, as a way of ensuring stability and nipping misunderstandings in the bud, engage in regular top-level meetings between the senior officials of universities and the colleges but inevitably such meetings tend to concentrate on operational matters. What is apparent is that reliance on market forces to shape the two sectors may have been successful in shaking out weaker constituents but needs re-consideration now not only to ensure stability but also to ensure that the student interest is respected and that the interests of society and the economy in continuing a pro-active process of widening participation through joint college and university collaboration is protected and, if possible, extended.

What is evident is the way the establishment of college networks and the recruitment of significant proportions of students through them imposes a regional character on a university: vice-chancellors or other senior officers find the need to be on the road to make regular visits to colleges, groups of academics become engaged in joint consultation with college staff over curriculum matters or on quality assurance issues, students are encouraged to look outwards from their college environments to the wider world of higher education. At Plymouth, where its network is large and has been in operation for many years, the University has built up a significant partnership office headed by a senior academic which has brought professionalism into the management of partnership arrangements. While university/college relationships may have been initiated for primarily student recruitment reasons the effect can be to turn universities into becoming regional players and to change the character of the institutions. Nowhere is this more true than amongst the post-post-1992 universities, Chester and Gloucestershire, previously teacher training based colleges of higher education or Lincoln University establishing itself in a region previously deprived of higher education. By adopting this regional dimension universities have transformed themselves and their regions, and the opportunities for progression into higher education, from what had existed before.

Chapter 5

The Impact of University Engagement on Regions

Changing priorities in local and regional relationships

It was implicit in the creation of the colleges in the nineteenth century, which became the civic universities of the twentieth, that universities should play a role in civic or regional development. Their science and technology departments collaborated closely with local industry and were regarded as part of the local economic landscape. They developed long-lasting relationships integral to the local economy. Thus, the Clothworkers' Company endowed both central buildings and academic departments relating to the woollen industry at the Yorkshire College of Science, the forerunner of the University of Leeds. The University still graduates its students in the Clothworkers' Great Hall, opened in 1894, and continues to maintain a research relationship with the Company. However, although throughout the subsequent period the government and the University Grants Committee strongly encouraged research and teaching links with industry and funded schemes to enhance them there was no comprehensive effort to seek to integrate universities into regional economic and social policies as there was in the Land Grant universities in the United States where public service was incorporated into universities' objectives with a weighting equal to that accorded to teaching and research.

Pre-1992 universities maintained good relations with local authorities but they became more ceremonial than operational. The focus of the UGC was institutional teaching and research, a perspective reinforced by the introduction of research assessment exercises in 1985–6. If anything, its focus moved away from the local and regional. In an attempt to encourage broader and more obviously economically and socially beneficial programmes in research, the government introduced the Higher Education Innovation Fund (HEIF) with the stated aim of creating and sustaining knowledge exchange activities with business, public and third sector organizations and community bodies. But although characterized as creating 'third leg' activities, this remained a sideshow and never challenged the priority given to research which qualified for ranking and funding in the research assessment exercises. In particular, it remained a central initiative with no explicit regional criteria built into the decision-making.

A different set of circumstances affected the polytechnics/post-1992 universities. They had developed on the basis of full time and part time degree and sub degree programmes and were never routinely funded for non-credentialized ('extra mural') education. Although from their creation they were functionally very close to the local authorities, relationships were damaged by the controls, bureaucratic and political, which the latter exercised over them. Moreover, most local authorities tended to restrict their interests narrowly to their own immediate civic boundaries. For most polytechnics, the 1988 legislation which transferred them (in England and Wales) from local authority to central government control constituted a release from relationships which had gone sour. Relations improved, however, in the next decade and with the availability of European Regional Development Grants (ERDF) for eligible authorities, partnerships between universities and local authorities to upgrade city centres and university facilities as part of a package, became common. Cooperation and collaboration became more general but continued to fall short of genuinely disinterested programmes designed to regenerate local and regional economies. The fact that further education remained controlled centrally in England, like the universities, imposed a further limitation on longer term joint planning, together with the added complexity for universities of adjusting to the risks of a funding regime dependent on tuition fee income. Coherent urban or regional planning which incorporates further and higher education has been difficult to achieve. The mood now seems to have changed but the machinery to implement regional policies involving all the main players has yet to be put in place.

The most substantial step away from local and regional engagement, the significance of which went largely unnoticed at the time, was the withdrawal of funding for 'extra mural studies' in the pre-1992 universities in the mid 1980s.

These departments, running classes, evening, day and weekend, aimed at the community, represented a key element in the relationships between universities and their regions. In the US, Sorber shows how the growth of extension programmes came to complement the rest of the Land Grant programmes (Sorber 2018: 138–49). In the UK 'extra-mural' departments had had a long history. First introduced by Cambridge in the 1850s, the practice of offering programmes of non-credentialed courses to the public, particularly in industrial areas or areas of social or economic hardship became general amongst the original civic universities up to the founding of the 1960s New Universities. (Oxford passed responsibility for its programmes in Brighton and East Sussex to the new University of Sussex when that university was established.) Funding for these programmes in the UK system was provided direct from the Department of Education and Science (DES) which made universities 'responsible bodies' for the funding stream. Responsible body funding had a strong element of head count in it and was subject to a degree of complexity over student participants which in most universities only the director of extra mural studies fully understood. However, the system had the benefit of earmarking the resources made available and isolating it from UGC funding so giving the departments great freedom in piloting their futures. A key element in these programmes was outreach so that universities located extra mural tutors in university adult education centres containing classrooms and some social facilities at selected sites in their region. Leeds, for example, which had a large department with its own building on the periphery of the main campus, had centres as far afield as Bradford, Middlesbrough, Pateley Bridge and Scarborough, and served an area strikingly congruent to the future West Yorkshire Combined Authority region. In fact, it exhibited a more than passing resemblance to the kind of US extension programme implied by the Wisconsin slogan, 'the boundaries of the University are the boundaries of the State'. Such centres were not only valuable educationally but also acted as key university nodes into the communities creating two-way information flows as well as encouraging a modest market of mature students.

All this was brought to an end not as the result of any great debate about the regional role of universities or their responsibilities for widening participation but as a result of thoughtless bureaucratic rationalizations in the aftermath of the 1981 cuts in university budgets and the continuing reductions in the financing of the university system in the 1980s. The first step was to consolidate a reduced DES grant into the normal UGC university financing arrangements thus removing the protection for extra mural budgets within university resource allocation processes and opening them up to internal competition for resources at the very time when research assessment pressures and overall reductions in grant were imposing staff reductions across the board. The second step was more fundamental to amend the original student numbers formula used for the DES allocation to cover credentialized courses only, in other words courses which involved written work and end of course assessment and which led to the award of a recognized sub degree qualification and to require that they became self-financing. At a stroke this removed funding for the standard extra mural evening class in the humanities and related fields in favour of vocational short courses for which tuition fees were chargeable. One argument justifying the decision was to remove supposed overlaps between university, local authority and Workers' Educational Association (WEA) courses; another was the clear priority which the government (or the Treasury) gave to vocational and professional short courses over the liberal arts biases perceived in the extramural programmes. The result was the effective end of the extra mural movement with the inevitable redundancies imposed on extra mural tutors being lost in the parallel fall out amongst discipline-based academics as a result of the research assessment exercises. Old style extra mural departments, with their regional centres, only survived as centralized departments of continuing education, regionally based adult education centres were closed and the opportunity was lost to build on their expertise and relationships to develop broader sustainable regional links (Jones et al. 2010). Indeed, to the communities involved it looked as if the universities were withdrawing from these relationships.

The impact of universities on their regions remains very much determined by their disciplinary strengths which have been shaped by their histories and by their locations: research-led universities with strong science and technology departments and medical schools located in major cities link naturally with industry in their area; teaching-led universities are much more concerned with social regeneration, widening participation and relations with the public sector of the economy, welfare state services where labour shortages amongst the professions are crucial to a sustainable regional economy. The activities led by research-led universities tend towards business and technological development; those led by teaching-led universities tend towards meeting the personal demands of public services under strain. The differentiation is not rigid: both Leeds and Newcastle Universities have major medical schools which are key contributors to the public medical services in their regions while universities like Birmingham City and Plymouth make significant contributions to industry in their areas. But the bigger picture is that because of the absence of investment in their disciplinary base comparable to that inherited by the older universities, the post-1992 universities tilt in their contribution towards the public sector while the pre-1992 universities' strengths point them much more towards the private sector or to large-scale joint public and private sector capital-intensive projects. The following section describes the differences in universities' strategies towards engagement.

Universities' engagement strategies

It is not surprising that universities play to what they regard as their strengths as well as to the opportunities provided by the market. Leeds University with its long history of research partnership with local and regional industry, its powerful medical school and its location in the middle of a prosperous city has been a natural driver both for economic and cultural development in the city. It has played a substantial role in helping the West Yorkshire Combined Authority and the Leeds City Enterprise Partnership (the LEP) to develop their industrial strategy particularly in areas like healthcare, digital health and in health technologies. It has bought into, in conjunction with the City, KPMG and other local bodies, an MIT consultancy, the MIT Regional Entrepreneurship Acceleration Programme (REAP), to create a regional development programme aimed at SMEs, and, again in partnership it has created the NEXUS enterprise and innovation centre, a £40m building next-door to the University

> 'that brings the business community, large corporates down to very small- and medium-sized businesses into the university and links them up with researchers who are working in areas of interest which might be healthcare, engineering, environmental sciences and so on'. (1)

attracting companies from as far away as Canada and Asia to become tenants. Additionally, the building houses the University's own Research and Innovation Services Office and the Government's Transport Catapult Centre, and acts as a hub for student entrepreneurs. As a city, Leeds could be said to be on the crest of a wave with selection as the northern site for the Bank of England, the new home of Channel 4, the location of NHS Digital and, with Opera North, Northern Ballet, an international piano competition, major theatres, museums and galleries; it is confirming its role as a powerful regional city. On the one hand, as one senior academic said:

> 'as a Russell Group university we have to be really clear that we recognize the strength of fundamental research and the importance of it to deliver things that may seem sort of isolated at the moment but which could actually be the discovery that shapes the world in thirty years' time.' (2)

Such a mission, however, must also include a relationship with the city and with business recognizing that:

> 'we have the duty, a responsibility, to put something always back into the city … if it wasn't for the city, and as you will remember from history, the clothworkers, there wouldn't be a university in Leeds.' (3)

A coincidence, as far as this study is concerned, is that Newcastle University was also advised through the North East LEP by the MIT REAP consultancy and has pursued a broad strategy which has much in common with Leeds. Its major contribution is the Helix, a twenty-four-acre site in the heart of the city, an innovation hub like NEXUS, its title intended to represent 'the quadruple Helix of the university, local government, business and the community' (4). Newcastle, however, has a long history of regional engagement including the re-creation, as public facilities on the campus, of the Great North Museum and the Halton Art Gallery, while its medical school has a reach that extends throughout the north-east. The Helix itself is the successor of a Science City project and is seen as the physical manifestation of the University's strategy towards collaboration with its key partners the City Council and the North East Regional Health Authority, combining academic research centres, teaching facilities and locations for businesses. Its brochure states that its vision is:

> 'to create a destination that attracts global talent, harnesses the intellectual horsepower from the University and taps into the drive from the Council to create economic growth in the city and lasting change'. (*Newcastle Helix: A new home for innovation and business in the centre of Newcastle* 2021)

The University illustrates very clearly the tensions of being a research university and playing a leading local and regional role. It argues that it can combine globally-related research based on issues arising out of the city and its region with a strong emphasis on community engagement. But like Leeds it has post-1992 universities, Northumbria and Sunderland Universities, sitting close beside it within the city encouraging a voluntary determination of roles. This reinforces the differentiation of the research intensive, Newcastle University, from the research active, Northumbria and Sunderland Universities, and influences its strategy towards widening participation. Thus it recognizes that children in the north east 'are less likely to go to university than anywhere else in the country and that has to reflect what we know about the levels of education, the levels of social deprivation up here' (5), but in its collaboration with schools its policy is to look for the 'brightest' children from disadvantaged backgrounds rather than seeking more general partnerships for student progression with local further education colleges. It differentiates its approach to apprenticeship degrees by selecting subject areas like 'computer data, cybersecurity, power engineering, things where we are research-wise internationally leading and if you are going to do a cybersecurity course, which everyone needs for their companies, why not do it at a place that majors in research in that?' (6) a sharp contrast with the extensive apprenticeship programmes in non-science and technological fields in nursing, police training, healthcare and social work at, for example, the University of Chester.

The circumstances of their location in city centres and in proximity to industry (more so in Leeds than in Newcastle), together with their histories, shapes the Universities of Leeds and Newcastle, and the character of their engagement with their communities in very particular ways. Lancaster and Stirling Universities, though cut from the same cloth of formation under the UGC policy framework, lack the local characteristics which determine the profile of Leeds and Newcastle. They are campus universities developed on semi-rural sites on the periphery of small towns; they are both notable for the lack of any significant kind of local or regional industrial interface. (A senior member of staff at Lancaster commented: 'if I leave the campus I'm in fields with sheep', very different from the environment of his former city centre university (7)). Lancaster is a successful university but not because of its particular engagement with its region. This is not because of reluctance on its part but because of an absence of large organizations to partner with. It has a small, and new, medical school and nursing degrees which connect it to the NHS and local hospitals. It has a centre devoted to Ruskin, the nineteenth century Lake District writer, philosopher and art critic, and it is deeply involved with the creation of Eden International, the planned expansion from the Eden Project in Cornwall to be sited in the Morecambe Bay area, but its main industrial links and relationships with commerce are outside its region. A similar situation exists in Stirling where the University works closely with the regional health board, NHS Forth Valley, in relation to nurse and midwife training and research in regional population health and community health and has an innovation park housing some fifty companies but its most notable areas of research in aquaculture and global food security (for which it won a Queen's Award), river estuary management, and dementia, are nationally or internationally engaged rather than locally or regionally though support for the aquaculture programme was included in the Towns Fund application. As one interviewee reported:

> 'Stirling has always had an applied focus to the work that we've done; we were founded with the strong professional part of our portfolio so with teachers, with nurses and midwives, with social workers we've always been targeting our approach; our science has tended to have an applied focus'. (8)

but in the absence of a substantial urban and industrial infrastructure it cannot compete on equal terms, particularly in the major sciences and technologies, with the older Scottish universities. The physical contributions of both universities to their regions, apart from the campuses themselves, are therefore more limited although their national and international impact in specialist areas is considerable.

This contrasts with the contributions of our four immediately post-1992 universities (Birmingham City, East London, Plymouth, and South Wales Universities) with their strongly urban heritages. With the expansion of their student numbers their new buildings have contributed to the transformation of their urban settings, while in the case of Birmingham City, Plymouth and South Wales their contribution to the cultural life of their cities through the Birmingham Conservatoire and the Welsh School of Music and Drama, both institutions joining the universities as part of rationalizing mergers, and the Plymouth cultural quarter has been considerable. In themselves, these have made transformational impacts on their city centres in terms of the physical development of concert halls, theatres, museums, art galleries and teaching facilities comparable in terms of footprint to the impacts of Nexus and the Helix in Leeds and Newcastle. Plymouth and South Wales have also made significant scientific and industrial contributions to their regions. Plymouth, which started life in the nineteenth century as a school of navigation, is a leading university in marine engineering and has won a Queen's Award for its marine science. It works closely with the Royal Devonport Dockyard and Babcock Marine and leads the national EPSRC Supergen national consortium on offshore renewables. The University of South Wales works closely with GE Aviation Wales (which is only a mile from the Pontypridd campus) one of the most prominent aircraft maintenance companies in the world and the largest industrial company in Wales, and with the Tata Steel company. It also works with the CBI and the Federation of Small Businesses in respect to SMEs. Conversely, the University of East London is benefitting from London's movement eastwards so that it is now located close to the Lord Mayor's Office with the headquarters of HM Customs and Excise in nearby Southwark, and has developed relationships with Siemens and Amazon Web Services. The opportunities for alignment with companies moving into proximity with the University are growing sharply from the depressed state of the East End a decade ago. Previously sited in an area of extreme poverty the university is finding the environment lifted by affluent commercial incomers with whom it hopes through partnerships and joint activities it can intensify its role in education, training and in research. As an indication of how its region is changing, however, it continues to have a close link with the Newham Community Group, the largest foodbank provider in the UK.

If we turn now to our four post-post-1992 case study institutions, we find that their contributions to their regions are much more differentiated than those of the earlier foundations. One would have expected, for example, that the two former teacher-training institutions might have followed a common approach in relation to their regions especially when their teacher-training curriculum limited them, as it did, from investing in significant scientific and technological fields. Both were in relatively affluent towns but were faced with the challenge that to compete with the rest of the higher education sector they had to diversify which meant stepping out from the restricted range of disciplines and recruitments markets they were used to. In practice, they opted for very difference strategies: Gloucestershire chose to develop a new campus in Gloucester attuned much more closely to Gloucester's very different needs but to limit its territorial reach to the county of Gloucestershire itself and to adopt a cautious approach to disciplinary diversification. Chester on the other hand, with a much broader and more diverse region to confront, chose to open up satellite facilities in Warrington and Shrewsbury and to engage with the huge chemical industry which operates around the Mersey in the north of Cheshire. It has established a science park adjacent to Stanlow Oil Refinery and has ambitions to establish itself in the new hydrogen economy. With plans to develop a full campus in Warrington and to increase the student population in both Warrington and Shrewsbury coupled with an energetic policy of widening its recruitment policy, Chester has moved a long way from its more cloistered past. It would be easy to regard this as a more positive approach than has been adopted in Gloucestershire, but this would be to ignore the considerable task of developing a full Gloucester campus, which has been achieved, and running two campuses as a unitary institution despite the awkward relationship between the two local authorities. Both universities have worked very closely with their local communities in designing new and relevant curricula, aligning their strategies closely with their LEPs, and both see themselves as driven by their communities' needs but the institutional outcomes are very different because the opportunities that their regions present for growth and development are very different.

The contributions made by Lincoln and the Highlands and Islands Universities are different again and are among the most distinctive in their approaches of any universities in the UK. The Highlands and Islands University represents the solution to an otherwise difficult geographical problem: how to provide higher education opportunities to a sparsely populated region where population centres are not large enough to develop comprehensive institutions on their own. The University has succeeded brilliantly in marshalling the various town-based further education colleges and the more remote research organizations into a coherent university structure. The data recorded in Chapter 3 show that it has met the ambition of its founders to provide a disincentive to migration out of the region to attend the older Scottish universities in the economically more advanced south. Moreover, it has broken the UK mould in being genuinely comprehensive, in that the University is funded for both further and higher education.

If the Highlands and Islands University is distinctive in the way it is constructed to meet its region's needs, Lincoln has also trodden a very different path to other post-post-1992 universities. Transferring from Hull to Lincoln it occupied a campus created for it in the heart of the city. However, unlike the New Universities in the 1960s, the site was urban not semi-rural and the stated objective was the regeneration of Lincoln itself, an objective which it eventually enlarged to the much larger region described in Chapter 2. Unlike Lancaster and Stirling, it lacked any of the in-built disciplinary investment or financial support provided by the UGC in the 1960s. To make any kind of impact it had to 'work with the assets that you have and you develop research for those assets, and you then become distinctive but globally recognized' (9). An opportunity for the application of this self-help approach appeared quite early in the University's life with the decision of Siemens to pull out of the city because it was unable to recruit graduate engineers. The University persuaded Siemens to give support to the establishment of an engineering department and a decade later Siemens and the University co-located in a new engineering building on the campus, Siemens has expanded its Lincoln operation and has retained its graduate recruitment from the University; the supply chain network has also benefitted. Working with the Lincolnshire Cooperative Society, which operates a substantial chain of pharmacies, the University has founded a School of Pharmacy and has created a science park. Working with hospitals it has created degrees in nursing, physiotherapy and paramedic science leading to the creation of a medical school validated by the long-established medical school at Nottingham. Working with a prosperous farming community it has developed what it claims to be the largest agri-robotics team in Europe. It has adopted a similar approach to building a cultural presence. Unlike the pre-1992 universities it has built working with employers into all its degree programmes thus emphasizing employability issues and binding employers into their relationship with the University.

Lincoln provides a particular contrast to the 1960s campus universities because unlike them sustained by a programme of promised investment in a given range of fields decided by the state, it has had to be entrepreneurial in developing its interests in conjunction with the opportunities that its region offered. If Lincoln was the New University of the 2010s, it was driven by a very different set of ideas to the New Universities of the 1960s – it was leaner, much more integrated with its community and region, not at all feeling the need to model itself on the much older civic universities. This is not at all to disparage the achievements of the 1960s institutions but simply to underline the differences in the climate that brought them into being and the changes which this has imposed on the character of the institutions and their impact on their regions.

Region, history and institutional mission

As we have seen, the higher educational institutional landscape is substantially differentiated by two factors: changes in national policy deriving mostly from the continuous growth in student numbers and its financial implications and the impact of regional differences which can have a determining influence on institutional strategies. The four sets of institutional types described in this study, the Russell Group civics, the 1960s New Universities, the post-1992 urban universities and the post-2000 group of universities, were shaped, in descending order, by an increasing concentration in the provision of support for STEM subjects in a restricted number of universities. The civic universities were heavily endowed with science and technology support from before and after the Second World War and benefitted disproportionally from the results of the research assessment exercises from the mid-1980s. With their location in the centre of large cities they were well placed to work creatively with industry and, when the time came, to partner their cities to revive city centres while at the same time acquiring more space for scientific and technological research advances of their own. The 1960s campus universities, which were seen primarily by the UGC as a response to the rising student numbers that were anticipated by the Robbins Report, were essentially short-changed in pump-priming funding for STEM subjects because of the costs involved and the doubts about size of the student market in these fields; the student number swing away from science prevented a substantial build-up in science and technological research over the next two decades except in specialist areas. Their regions also lacked the industrial infrastructure which could have prompted the development of depth in STEM subjects. In 1992, when the polytechnics became universities they entered the first research assessment exercise with no background in dual funding as polytechnics and with STEM departments geared as much towards non-degree as to degree work (the University of Central England, now Birmingham City University did not even submit a bid to the 1992 research assessment exercise). As Plymouth and South Wales Universities demonstrate, some post-1992 universities have found it possible to develop secure long-term partnerships with industry but inevitably in a competitive market where the REF supports the strongest universities, the post-1992 universities are outgunned by the civics in winning major contracts which would enable them to build up their subject strengths. This leaves the post-post-1992 universities as being the least well supported in terms of STEM infrastructure for the most part initially reliant on the staffing and facilities appropriate to their teacher training background. This imposed severe limitations on their ability to develop partnerships with industry and pre-determined the balance of their regional engagement towards labour requirements in social and health fields. Lincoln's ability to grow its own engineering school on the back of its relationship with a large company is both a remarkable example of self-help and an indictment of a failure of national policy. Implicit in the decision to promote colleges of higher education to university status was that their future and their usefulness to society would be determined by the market but from a regional perspective this was to launch them without the wherewithal to play a more balanced role in the economics of their regional communities.

We should not be surprised therefore that the contributions of so many universities to their regions are primarily in the public sector of the economy – nursing, social care, social work, police studies – rather than in industrial or commercial fields. Here the great driver has been the student market particularly after the cap was taken off student numbers in England, Wales and Northern Ireland. The market as a method of managing higher education is certainly not without its critics, especially after the introduction of full-cost tuition fees in 2012, but the incentive it gave to partnerships with further education colleges and widening participation schemes should be recognized. (It could logically be argued that simply increasing the tuition fee component of the 2005 decision to charge up to £3,000 on top of recurrent grant might well have had the same effect as raising fee levels to full cost if it had been combined with the removal of the cap.) Nothing can disguise the fact that while urban centres containing Russell Group civic universities have potentially benefitted considerably from the joint investment in innovation hubs like Nexus and the Helix, perhaps the greatest regional beneficiary from university enterprise in the last decade has been the NHS in terms of nursing, paramedical degrees and the establishment of new medical schools in some post-1992 universities. Here the combined effect of Brexit, Covid-19 and the deterioration of health indices in some parts of the country has put the labour market outcomes of these courses centre stage in the operation of national medical services. It is easy to undervalue this aspect of universities' contributions to their regions, not least because it is made by universities that do not necessarily rate highly in national rankings, but social historians of the future may regard it as the more outstanding response.

What this chapter has tried to do is to draw a picture of the way different types of university have responded to different sorts of regional stimuli. It is clear that regions have had a decisive impact on universities' development strategies encouraging them to embark on ventures which may or may not be of long-term benefit to the institution and which have involved risk. What is also clear is that universities have widely differentiated strengths and weaknesses in responding to regional needs and that it is important both at national and regional levels that these differentiations are recognized and respected and built into policy. Innovation hubs in city centres driven by universities with significant investments in STEM subjects may make political and economic headlines but should also be balanced against the slower impact of educational advance into low-participation areas of economic and social deprivation or the maintenance of recruitment targets in NHS hospitals in unfashionable areas.

Chapter 6

Institutional Governance and Regional Strategy-making

The changing shape of institutional governance

The initiative for founding the original civic universities was local and regional not national. Leeds University, for example, was founded in 1874 as the Yorkshire College of Science by a group of citizens concerned about the extent to which the UK appeared to be falling behind the continent in technical education. These universities, as they became, were locally founded and the constitution of their governance while guaranteeing university autonomy nevertheless reflected both strong local community representation and the economic interests of the locality. The latter were transmitted through a court, a large heterogeneous body made up of local representatives and local donors not unlike a mediaeval *parlement* which met annually to receive a report from the vice-chancellor, and a smaller 'executive governing body', the council, which was legally responsible for the business side of the university, in particular its finance and estate. A typical council would be made up of thirty-five to forty members, the majority external to the university (the lay members); the court might involve some 150 members, mostly representative of local institutions including local authorities. The court appointed the university's chancellor, an honorary appointment only, but some courts also retained residual powers to take decisions which would otherwise be taken by councils. Their main function, as universities developed, was to be the mouthpiece of the local community and there could thus be occasional tensions between views expressed locally about the university's activities and the university's own commitment to its national and international objectives, largely the concern of the academic senate.

In these early days, the universities were self-financing, supporting themselves substantially from tuition fees, and contributions from communities and short-term grants from HM Treasury. The creation of a University Grants Committee (UGC) in 1919 brought some funding stability but also began the process of centralizing policy towards the universities and reducing local and regional involvement which has continued to this day (Shattock 2012). Although between 1919 and 1939 UGC funding made up only about 30 per cent of an institution's budget, leaving much of the remainder to come from local sources, central policy-making in areas like science and technology or medicine became nationally important. In 1946, the financial consequences of the Second World War for the universities compelled the government to, in effect, take over the whole funding of the university system, a position that continued until 2000 when the introduction of a tuition fee of £1,000 marked the first very cautious step by the state to supplement recurrent grant made from central sources with contributions from the student market, a process which was to culminate in 2012 with the removal of recurrent grant altogether, except for supplementary support for STEM subjects, and with the substitution of full-cost tuition fees in a student dominated market.

Throughout this long period of evolution, the role of central government, as evidenced by the controls exercised by the UGC, the Higher Education Funding Councils and, in England from 2018, the Office for Students, increased at the expense of local or regional interests. It was perhaps inevitable that with the UGC responsible for the major proportion of university funding, the financial and ultimately the controlling function of university councils diminished. University councils were relieved of the active fund-raising role expected of them up to the Second World War and their lay membership, almost entirely local, became increasingly distanced from critical decision-making which devolved itself to the vice-chancellor and the senate. The first sign of change was the impact of the 1981 cuts in government expenditure and the Jarratt Committee's call for university councils to become more effective and 'to assert themselves', presumably in respect to their vice-chancellors and senates, though this was never spelt out, and for universities to be less bureaucratic and more efficient (CVCP, Jarratt Report 1985).

The Report received strong backing from the UGC which required universities to present reports on the steps they had taken to implement the recommendations. Most universities responded by seeking changes to their statutes to reduce the size of their councils removing local authority representatives, who had become largely passengers, and by abolishing their courts which had seemingly lost their usefulness and had become occasions devoted mostly to institutional self-congratulation and public relations, on the grounds that it improved efficiency and reduced bureaucracy. Twelve years later, the Dearing Committee, reflecting government thinking, called for a further reduction in council membership to improve their decision-making capacity and for governing bodies to 'take responsibility for the institutions' strategic direction' (Dearing Report 1997: para 15–33). Subsequent amendments to accountability requirements continued to strengthen governing bodies' responsibilities to government; the need for them to exercise a strong strategic role was re-emphasized. This required them to act increasingly like a company managing board. Shattock and Horvath describe this as the 'business model' of corporate governance (Shattock and Horvath 2019: 165). This put pressure on universities to lay stress on seeking governors who could best match these requirements, senior industrialists and professionals, usually to be recruited nationally, who would bring strategy and accountability to the table rather than any specialist knowledge of or sensitivity towards local or regional issues.

Meantime, a further giant step in centralization had been the transfer of the polytechnics from local government to central government control in 1988, a move which was substantially undertaken because of the extent to which an expanding set of polytechnics had outgrown the ability of local governments to exercise effective governance over them but also to strengthen central government control. When the polytechnics were 'nationalized' the Department for Education and Science (DES) appealed for and obtained a list of candidates for lay membership of their governing bodies replacing the almost universal local membership. Very few of these new members had regional interests and almost none had local authority connections.

After it changed to university status, De Montfort University set the pace by consistently seeking 'the great and the good' to be members, irrespective of where they were based, in an effort to reposition the University into an imagined higher university league. Many other post-1992 and quite a few pre-1992 universities followed suit. Subsequently and over time, the effect of the repeated research assessment exercises and the influence of league tables and ranking systems and, post 2012 when the student number cap was removed, the emergence of a competitive higher education funding market based on open-ended student recruitment, all conspired to persuade universities to turn away from local and regional concerns and to concentrate their attention on national targets and national priorities. The state itself did nothing to discourage this and became increasingly interventionist, thus further distancing institutions from local or regional interests. It would be wrong to imply that individual universities did not launch regional engagement projects over this period but long-term university relationships with local government were much reduced, or became of only formal importance, while their priorities became increasingly to satisfy mandates laid down by central government. The evidence provided by the previous chapters suggests that for many universities these priorities are changing: local and regional institutional engagement is becoming of much greater importance for general economic and social reasons as well as for institutional development. The question arises as to whether institutional governance structures should not reflect these changes.

Institutional governance practice and regional engagement

The UK institutional governance model prior to 1992 was bicameral with a governing body (council) and a senate elected from within the university. The council, as the 'executive governing body', was responsible for finance, capital development and management, the senate for academic matters but with a 'shared' role in the management of the institution. Strategy, in so far as it was a formal function, was the business of both senate and council. The legislation covering universities founded after 1992 amended this to a unicameral structure with authority being firmly transferred from academic boards to governing bodies (boards of governors) and with management and planning functions being vested in the vice-chancellor as chief executive, answerable only to the governing body. In practice, over time the constitutions of pre- and post-1992 foundations have come together. The constitutional sovereignty of the governing body has been greatly strengthened and the membership has been reduced in size ensuring a greater proportionate representation of lay members. The appointment of lay membership is subject to recommendations from a nominations committee appointed by the governing body itself. It can be argued that this has a self-perpetuating effect on the style of membership though in practice the vice-chancellor normally represents the leading voice in selecting names for recommendation. The reduction in the governance and management role of senates and academic boards has been paralleled by the rise of an executive (either simply as a body of senior officers or as a constituted executive board) which is answerable to the governing body through a vice-chancellor acting as chief executive (Shattock and Horvath 2019). The Committee of University Chairs' (CUC) Code of Higher Education Governance states that:

> 'Working with the Executive the governing body sets the mission, strategic direction, overall aims and values of the institutions. In ensuring the sustainability of the institution the governing body actively seeks and receives assurance that delivery of the strategic plan is in line with legislative and regulatory requirements, institutional values, policies and procedures and there are effective systems of control and risk management in place.' (CUC Code 2020)

In addition, governing bodies are, of course, the financially accountable bodies to central government authorities.

This structure has emerged from the conditions of the last quarter of a century and in the light of considerable prompting from central government sources. The question now to be asked is whether it remains appropriate in the light of universities' growing engagement with local regional economies and their impact as one of many agencies operating at these levels on programmes of urban and rural regeneration and industrial development. Can lay members of governing bodies adequately reflect the public interest in regional development as well as their universities' own interests especially when a high proportion are recruited on a national basis and indeed should they seek to? If not, who should?

The evidence from our research suggests that some consideration needs to be given to the role of governing bodies, and particularly to that of the lay majority, in respect of the extent to which universities are now becoming involved as leading actors in community action, regional engagement and in public and private partnerships aimed at economic development. We found that our case study institutions in practice had very similar governing body structures and approaches whether their constitutions were of pre- or post-1992 origins. The average size of their membership was twenty, with twenty-five the largest and sixteen the smallest, as compared to the figure of thirty-five to forty before the effect of the recommendations of the Jarratt Report took effect in the late 1980s on the pre-1992 universities. Membership is predominantly lay with academic and other staff and student representation being only a small minority. While a few universities reserve a place for members with particular backgrounds – a politician, a former vice-chancellor, a representative of a charity or of a collaborating NHS Trust – the great majority of members are drawn from business and within that from people who have accounting or finance backgrounds, reflecting university concern with regard to national pressures on financial accountability and financial management in continuing periods of financial turbulence.

The commonality in the style of membership may be summarized in comments from a pre-1992 and a post-1992-university:

> 'we try and get pretty much legal, financial, property and business, they are the sort of areas we would go for in our lay members.' (1)

> 'they are, I think, very much that classic polytechnic board of governors. There's an awful lot of accountants, a scattering of lawyers, former chief executives of FTSE One Hundred companies.' (2)

Where interesting differences in selection policy appeared was in respect to the locations of their lay members. Only one university emphasized the importance it placed on this:

> 'we deliberately try to get in people not just who live here but people who have important professional networks here.' (3)

Against this, several universities were sceptical of local as compared to broader metropolitan approaches to governor recruitment:

> 'The board was terribly local. I mean they never went anywhere to recruit other than to their local friends . . . we don't choose anyone because they live in the region, we choose people based on their skills.' (4)

> 'everyone on the board lived locally. I tried to get more diversity within that'. (5)

Universities gave different reasons for widening their recruitment: 'Very local, pretty well all local' so the university concerned used head-hunters to identify 'people who have worked in a bigger something with a bigger scope' (6). Another took a conscious decision to move away from a locally dominated membership which, it was concerned, generated too 'parochial' a view to around half being drawn from national roles:

> 'We needed to have a governing body where people had similar horizons and understandings of the complexity as well as being able to potentially draw on networks, etc.' (7)

Two universities explicitly excluded the benefit of living in the locality or region as a criterion for recruitment. One university which had a split of half and half between regionally and nationally based lay governors referred to the latter as 'people who typically travel up from London to sit on our council' (8). An inevitable consequence was that lay members living in the locality had to take a larger share of committee work where detailed consideration of policy issues was more likely to take place. This is not to say that in appointing people from metropolitan settings universities did not take account of local connections, often alumni, but the fact that they had a metropolitan background was the major criterion.

It is not surprising, therefore, that governing bodies are less interested and less expert in contributing to regional engagement policy:

> 'I wouldn't describe our lay members as being a strong driver in terms of regional engagement ... the desire to engage is growing but I would describe it as developing.' (9)

> 'I wouldn't say there was a collective university council view of regional engagement and development. But there is a very clear collective and active view amongst the senior people in the university.' (10)

> 'The governing body doesn't have any influence really on that strategic direction [regional engagement]. They approve the strategy and adopt it but I've never heard them talk about the region in that sense as being important.' (11)

> 'I think I'm probably ahead of them in understanding how significant the university could be [in its regional engagement]. What they worry still about are – I don't know – adverse news stories or that sort of thing ... And what

> I'm trying to do is step back and say to them: why does this matter to the university, why is it a good idea if we get involved in this particular sector?' (12)

> 'Our anchor responsibility is absolutely embedded as a priority in our board of governors' ... but the 'regional development push comes more from the executive.' (13)

Perhaps the most striking finding is the apparent absence of the 'strategic direction' highlighted in the CUC Code quoted above:

> 'We've got a great chairman ... and he's very clear on what the role of a governing body is, it's there to keep an eye on the finances and to watch your reputation and check that you are doing what you say in your strategy.' (14)

> 'It's my job to produce a strategy for the board to consider and approve ... So, it becomes our plan, it's not them pushing us and it's not us pushing them but there is a challenge about how we are delivering'. (15)

Because the governing body is made up the way it is:

> 'there is quite a lot of focus on ensuring that, yes, we understand that you are an educational charity, but that doesn't mean that you can't run it in an efficient way, and efficiencies can get overly interpreted as simply meaning business or corporate efficiency.' (16)

Is there a governance deficit?

The evidence, therefore, suggests that governing bodies are reliant for any role in strategy on the leadership of the vice-chancellor alone or on the wider executive. They approve, therefore, what is put before them perhaps arguing on some points of detail, but they do not 'direct'. Because a significant number of members are not local, their grasp of the detail of regional engagement issues is likely to be fairly sketchy. Moreover, in respect to these regional issues, a membership drawn from the financial and business community is not well placed to see a university's role from a regional economic or social perspective, but rather as to whether individual university ventures are appropriate to the interests of the institution itself and do not open it to unnecessary financial risk. There is little or no evidence that governing bodies, while they may approve strategy documents placed before them, have any overriding interests in regional engagement or are in a position to offer creative guidance on local or regional strategic issues or how they might affect the university's mission let alone be able to advise on how individual ventures might impact on local or regional interests. Only one university mentioned a wish to attract people with important local or regional professional networks.

Rather, the prevailing mood in universities appears to substitute a local contribution and involvement in governance in favour of 'metropolitan' figures supposedly better placed to bring broad experience to the counsels of a university. This may represent an undervaluing of the relevance of local and regional membership and the range of expertise, experience and community standing to draw on, and an underlying sense that their views may be more limiting and less useful in current circumstances than a metropolitan view. There is no evidence that this is actually the case. The fact that so many of the universities were using head-hunters to identify possible new members suggests that vice-chancellors and chairs of nomination committees have themselves been less involved in local and regional affairs to be able to identify individuals who would bring something to the table. For universities committed to regional engagement and particularly to local or regional regeneration it seems almost self-defeating to have to look for metropolitan figures of standing who by the nature of things will not be able to attend committees where the detailed work of governance takes place and who will only understand at second or third hand local or regional issues under discussion.

What is clear is that the initiative for regional engagement activity lies very much with a vice-chancellor, the executive and senior staff and that the governing bodies' roles are largely passive and reactive. As one vice-chancellor spelt out: 'they're there to keep any eye on us and make sure we're not doing silly things' (17), rather than to create or direct institution strategy. The approach to lay governance as currently conceived is strongly affected by national priorities and the emphasis placed on financial and other central accountabilities. The lay membership of a governing body made up primarily of people with financial or business backgrounds may play an important role in protecting a university from financial difficulties but may be less well suited to helping decide priorities over opening new rural centres, creating conditions whereby it can successfully partner established industrial enterprises or build structures which offer real support to small and medium sized enterprises. Most importantly, in the membership, one might expect to see people with real interest and professional backgrounds in regional affairs and, especially for those universities whose relationships are primarily with public sector professions and organizations, people from the health and social services who in their professional lives deal with very much the same kind of issues, including accountability, faced by universities. Regional engagement on the scale that it is now being practised needs to be reflected in the makeup of the lay component of governing bodies. The present model, which has emerged to reflect national and highly centralized policies in the 1990s and 2000s, needs to adapt to a situation where universities are seen to be crucial elements in programmes to relieve inequality within and between regions (the 'levelling up' agenda).

Our evidence suggests that the current arrangements for lay governance are no longer fit for purpose. As foregoing chapters indicate, universities have taken significant strides to pioneer new structures to contribute to this new agenda and governing bodies need to be aligned to support them. Moreover, one of the key features of the governance model adopted by the original civic universities and replicated in future foundations was that the presence of a lay majority on the governing body represented accountability to a wider public. They had a role in maintaining the independence of universities from incursions by government and in bridging relationships with their local communities. That role was exercised by members who were locally based, drawn primarily from the professions but broadly representative of community organizational networks and knowledgeable about local and regional affairs. The establishment of the university system as a tuition-fee-funded market (except in Scotland) has imposed a much greater competitive edge to the system. In a fragile economy, universities have to concentrate much more on their institutional self-interests and questions of public accountability, as distinct from specific financial accountability to central government, have appeared to be much less relevant. Nomination committees and head-hunters look for lay members who can enhance universities' prospects, introduce them to national networks and contribute national and international perspectives, rather than for improving local and regional relationships, and communication between university and civic and regional interests.

A larger element in this discussion, therefore, must be in the role of the regional community itself. Vice-chancellors and their executives are forging ahead with ambitious and enterprising plans for regional engagement primarily for institutionally self-interested reasons and without any formal overarching community oversight. In the past with governing bodies containing substantial local or regional representation there were local checks and balances which could be effective and which created machinery whereby conflicts of institutional and civic or societal interest could be addressed. The now disbanded courts of the pre-1992 universities, packed with local representation, provided a *post hoc* opportunity for widespread comment on the impact a university was having on its community. Courts were not executive bodies, except on very narrow issues, but local representatives took pride in their membership; membership conferred status locally and privileged access to the university. This is not to say that universities lack reference points with local or regional representative bodies. Many have close links with a LEP, have LEP members sitting on their governing bodies or the vice-chancellor is on the board of the local LEP; others have close relationships with local authority leaders – a Newcastle University senior officer chairs a Newcastle City Futures Board – but these may only provide a partial answer to the question as to how far the community has a place in guiding universities on priorities and assessing their contributions. For example, the LEPs are concerned to encourage economic growth and the creation of employment; they do not have a role in the social impacts of regeneration such as in the location of new further education facilities in areas where subsidies are required to make the schemes viable (although a government City Deal might have). The prestige university city's property development innovation hub needs to be considered not just from the enhancement of the city's prosperity but from the wider point of view of its impact on the economies of surrounding satellite town centres. Moreover, there might be benefits in local or regional coordination both to universities in identifying new opportunities but to the local and regional communities themselves.

These needs cannot be met by a simple reversion to the recruitment of a higher proportion of locally based lay members, although a broader range of public representation would match the activities and interests of universities more effectively than majorities made up of members drawn only from the business community. University governing bodies, vice-chancellors and university executive boards are necessarily concerned primarily with the progress of their own institutions but increasingly their impact on regional development requires a cross regional dialogue in which they should be playing a full part. This presupposes a substantial change in direction within regional bodies themselves and a change of balance between the authority of central policymaking and that of regional priorities giving greater initiative to regional decision-making.

Chapter 7

Regional Engagement and Universities: Some European Comparisons – Norway, Ireland and Germany

The question of regions and their place in the architecture of higher education has exercised many European countries, especially where, historically, universities were concentrated in a few affluent urban centres. In such countries, political pressures to provide equal opportunities for access to higher education in regions comparable to that in major cities has had profound effects on the structure of their higher education systems. Issues about the locus of authority and initiative, the balance between central and regional interests and about institutional autonomy became key elements in the policy agenda. In considering these questions in relation to the UK, and specifically England, it is useful to draw on the way they have been approached in some of these countries. Accordingly, contributions were commissioned from three countries, Norway, Ireland and Germany, which have addressed the issues of regional engagement and the centralization and decentralization of governance in different and contrasting ways. A discussion of these approaches and the relevance of their comparison is addressed in Chapter 8.

7.1 The regional factor in Norwegian higher education[1]

The Norway contribution begins with an account of the development of Norwegian higher education showing how the system was extended by legislation (the Quality Reform legislation) in 2003 to embrace a regional agenda. The second section describes how the system is governed, including the close partnership between the universities and the state, and how policy is driven by two key principles: that higher education should be equally accessible in all parts of the country and that any institution granted the title of university should be able to demonstrate a commitment to research. The third section emphasizes the national consensus regarding the political importance of the regional dimension in economic and social policy. The fourth section addresses the extent to which institutional governance is balanced between a board, the rector and the academic community while the final section uses the example of the requirement that every institution should establish a Council for Cooperation with Work Life as an illustration of how the balance between ministry policymaking and institutional autonomy can play out in practice.

Introduction: The development of regionality in the Norwegian university system

Norway has a population of 5.3 million comparable in size to that of Scotland and the Irish Republic; like other Scandinavian countries it is strongly committed to a welfare state and to education being seen as public good. Historically, universities were located in the south in the prosperous cities of Oslo, Bergen and Trondheim but in 1968 a decision was taken to establish a new university in Tromsø, which opened in 1972, explicitly to provide university education in the north of the country and to provide an alternative to student migration to the south for their higher education.

This was followed in 1994 by a plan to rationalize the ninety-eight regional colleges, some of which were as small as 100 students, into twenty-six university colleges. In 2003, the so-called Quality Reform legislation (St.meld, nr 27 2000–2001) incentivized a new wave of college mergers in which the prospect of achieving university status was offered if they satisfied criteria prescribed by the Norwegian Agency for Quality Assurance in Education (NOKUT), a new agency created as part of the reform process. NOKUT thus became a key agency in determining the shape of the higher education system and was given full authority to do so subject only to formal agreement by government (Bleiklie 2009; Maassen et al. 2011; Stensaker 2014).

There are now forty-seven higher education institutions, ten public comprehensive universities, six public specialized universities and thirty-one universities of applied science and university colleges. Acquiring full university status freed colleges from former local authority controls, although the regional bodies were not strong in any case, and gave them more autonomy within what was now a more centralized system. Mergers, which were voluntary though they had to be approved by NOKUT, did not involve campus closures but simply transferred authority from a single college to a new institution comprising two or more former colleges (in one case, as many as eight colleges); often these were some distance apart. The complexities of merging governance structures, deciding cross-institutional faculty structures or deciding that faculty structures should cohere with former college structures, resolving staffing implications and appropriate management hierarchies have taken time to settle down and make it difficult to assess even now the success of the process. This was particularly the case because of the impact of the 1994 rationalization of the college sector. One senior manager in a merged institution argued that:

> 'the university colleges did not really have a strategy; they did not really manage their own activities. They just grew. Because each year they were getting more money and more [funded] places and there were a lot of people who wanted to become a student so they just opened the doors ... it was not a strategy.' (1)

All higher education institutions have now entered a much more competitive environment.

The governance of the system

Responsibility for higher education is strongly centralized under the Ministry of Education and Research, although this is tempered by an equally high respect for institutional autonomy. Relations between the institutions and the Ministry are good although at the strategic level the Ministry drives the system. The structure provides that the Ministry sends each institution an annual allocation of resources letter, which includes student number targets, outlines overall objectives, and provides national indicators. Institutions respond with an annual report on the achievement of their objectives and submit an annual data return. The Ministry gives written feedback and every two years holds a governance dialogue with each institution. Policy interventions are conducted in a highly consensual manner and only after close consultation with the Rectors' Conference. Such consultations are not just for form but represent a 'very kind of dialogue oriented, consensus oriented' partnership (2). For example, a proposal from the Ministry to cluster the regional colleges into a limited number of large regional universities was criticized by the Rectors' Conference as being too radical a reform and the Ministry withdrew the proposal and substituted a scheme where incentive grants were offered to encourage voluntary institution-led mergers. In another case, the Ministry suggested that institutions should become independent self-owned corporations (the situation in many other countries, including the UK). This proposal was greeted with uproar by institutions which believed it to be a first step to marketizing the system as in the UK and the Ministry immediately withdrew the idea. The interplay between the Ministry and the Rectors' Conference is such that it can be argued that in most cases new proposals are shared between the two bodies. Philosophically, this springs from a common view that education is a public good and the idea that 'higher education is part of the society ... and part of the Nordic welfare state' (3). In particular, it incorporates the view that higher education should be accessible in all parts of the country and not just from a small group of institutions located in the more affluent parts.

A further determining principle of Norwegian higher education is that any institution granted the title of university or university of applied science should have a research commitment which should be assessed by NOKUT: a college should have at least four departments with doctoral programmes, individually approved by NOKUT, and have at least five different masters' programmes, and these programmes should each be taught by an appropriate number of doctorally qualified staff to qualify for a change of title. These qualifying requirements have imposed tough limitations on colleges' bids for university status and have involved significant academic and organizational challenges within the colleges themselves (Kyvik and Stensaker 2013). The ambition to qualify for university status, however, remains unabated.

The regional dimension

Our interviews in Norway impressed upon us the extent to which there was a national political consensus on the importance of regional policy and the extent to which opportunities available in the more affluent parts of the country should be equally available to citizens living elsewhere: 'the regional dimension is very important in Norwegian higher education' (4); 'regional politics in Norway overrides many other things' (5); 'I think the idea [of regional engagement] is primarily that regional politics in Norway is always really important, a sort of underlying argument in everything else also' (6). This consensus is very much reflected in Parliament where, when the Quality Reform legislation was being established, it was not the policy of a single party but was brought into existence by different coalition governments led by different political parties. Higher education policy was a largely uncontested area where there was general agreement that 'the sector was too fragmented, that there was a need for stronger institutions and higher quality' and that the higher quality should be combined with greater relevance to regional economies and societies (7). The decision in the Quality Reform process to encourage mergers was not driven by resource-based arguments but primarily to create larger units to ensure quality. One of the grounds for endowing NOKUT with such extensive powers in quality assurance in respect to mergers and the award of university titles was to enable expert professional assessment to bypass parliamentary involvement which would otherwise inevitably have invited interventions based on regional issues. A demonstration of the strength of Parliament's regional perspective is that a proposal that an individual campus in a particular merged institution should be closed on the grounds of financial viability and low student numbers has raised concerns within Parliament itself even though it has been supported by a local representative body.

Institutional governance

All Norwegian higher education institutions share a common governance structure of a governing board, a rector, a rector's executive committee, no senate but a commitment to strong academic governance at the faculty level. The governing board is made up of four external (lay) members appointed by the Ministry, four academic members elected from within the institution, a representative of the administrative staff and two students. In the Quality Reform process institutions were offered the choice of the rector remaining the chair of the board, the existing position in the older universities, with a formally appointed director of administration, or the chair being appointed from one of the external members with the rector acting as a quasi-chief executive. In the former structure, the rector was an elected position, in the latter an appointment by the board. In practice, the older universities, Oslo, Bergen, Trondheim and Tromsø opted to retain the rector's role as chair but in the newer institutions the alternative structure was preferred. In some institutions the rector is not a board member but this is a technical formality in that the rector would otherwise act in a chief executive role. Formally, although the Ministry appoints the external members, in practice it normally does so from a list submitted by the institution. Thus, the Ministry has the power to have direct influence over the governance of institutions but chooses not to exercise it.

How universities operationalize this structure is variable: the external members do not have a majority on the board, rectors' powers may in practice be limited by the views of powerful committees of deans or by faculties; a rector who chairs the board, as at Oslo, is clearly in a very different position to a rector of a newly created university where an external board member told us 'we instruct the rector, he is our man' (8). On the other hand a senior administrator from that institution argued that:

> 'we are not that dependent on the board; they have to start the strategy process and they have to take the final decisions but in reality much of the process is happening inside our organization,' (9)

and that the rector's powers were significantly circumscribed by the academic organs of governance:

> 'the level of academic freedom is very, very big and that means that even if the rector wants to change it is not always happening.' (10)

It is evident that, in spite of governance reforms, the role of the academic community remains very strong. It played a very significant role in some institutions in decisions over mergers; trades union pressures can be considerable, and a rector told us that he always checked a draft board agenda with the trade unions before formally issuing it to members. A lay board member, commenting on the role of the academic community, told us:

> 'We do not overrule something that is coming from the faculties … the board also has this respect for the local autonomy of the faculties.' (11)

Thus, in spite of the centralizing agencies of the Ministry and of NOKUT, institutions remain very much bottom-up organizations which have the power to resist successfully proposals they do not support.

The formation of Councils for Cooperation with Working Life

Following from the Quality Reform legislation, the Ministry issued a White Paper in 2008–9 (St.meld.nr 44 2008–2009) requiring institutions to establish Councils for Cooperation with Working Life in order to emphasize the expectation that institutions would be active in their engagement with localities and regions; this was incorporated into the allocation letters to institutions in 2011. An evaluation of the process and an assessment of its results was undertaken by the Nordic Institute for Studies in Innovation, Research and Education (NIFU) in 2017 and provides an interesting insight into the way the Norwegian higher education system operates and the interrelationships between central government and the institutions in a key policy area. The government's clear intention was to reinforce the Quality Reform legislation by the establishment of machinery which would ensure that the restructured institutional system would realize one of the key aims of the legislation which was to ensure that the institutions engaged with, and in their activities reflected, local and regional economies and cultures. Institutions were given flexibility as to whether they established self-standing Councils that would be advisory to rectors and boards of governors or whether to incorporate them into existing committee structures, but their composition had to include representatives of labour markets and students and might also include NGOs and elected officials. They were required both to develop an engagement strategy with clear goals and attainment targets and embed them into the institutions' strategies. They should also create a continuous dialogue with the labour market about the development of degree education and about the development of practical work in the curriculum. The Councils were also to set up panels for quality enhancement.

These were ambitious requirements to be made of autonomous institutions especially at a time when the sector was heavily involved in negotiations about mergers or the implementation of merger agreements. In some institutions, the establishment of a Work Life Council was overtaken by new merger agreements, in others where institutions had incorporated colleges at a considerable distance from one another the Council structure was devolved to individual campuses. A further difficulty was that local government was itself in the process of extensive reform leading to larger units which did not necessarily cohere with the regional distribution of university institutions so that local official representation on the Councils could be uneven and sporadic. In 2013, the Ministry checked on whether institutions had established the Councils and found that many had not done so or had responded with only minimal activities. On top of the administrative issues of timing there was also a strong feeling in many institutions that they already had regional engagement strategies and had no need to set up new machinery to create new ones. However, it became clear by the time of the NIFU review that the proposed reform 'didn't really take off' (12) and had not delivered the outcomes intended. According to the review, which was at pains not to be over critical of the Council idea, the existence of the Councils could be said to have added to strengthening dialogue at a strategic level but their impact on degree programmes was described in a summary of NIFU's 2017 report as being only 'modest' (13). The fact that the period for implementation clashed with a maximum administrative disruption in many institutions because of mergers and that mergers were also ongoing in local and regional authorities may have been relevant but does not fully explain, in a system so devoted to the regional interest, why more progress was not made. Perhaps the most telling explanation of the lack of impact of the proposed machinery can be found in the words of one person interviewed, not commenting directly on the fate of the Work Life proposal:

> 'that the regional dimension is somewhere in the decision sphere [for new courses] but it wouldn't be the case that ... it overrides any academic ideas on what would be an academic programme.' (14)

In other words, the saga of the introduction of the Councils for the Cooperation with Work Life, a clear expression of the Ministry's regional policies, reveals the limits of the Ministry's authority when academic issues are in play; essentially the academic community had seen off an attempt to pressurize it to override, as they saw it, academic policies with regional activities. The Norwegian system of governance of higher education balances centralization and direction with giving institutions autonomy and respect for academic decision-making. The Work Life proposals were fully in line with the Parliament's central concern over the primacy of the regional factor in policy making but the Quality Reform legislation also confirmed its acceptance of institutional autonomy which in practice permitted institutions to temporize over the Ministry's requirements in this case and in some cases simply to bury them within their own operations. It was not that they disagreed with the general aims of the Work Life proposals but that they represented an intervention into the internal management of the institution. The Ministry had already appointed members to institutional governing boards and boards had adopted strategies to achieve their own objectives which could be reviewed and commented on at biannual meetings with the Ministry, but the Work Life proposals represented a direct intervention in the decision-making of autonomous institutions. At senior management level in institutions the proposals were seen as adding little to what was already in process while at faculty level they looked dangerously intrusive into the academic control of the curriculum and the protection of academic freedoms in course development.

Conclusion

The Norwegian management of higher education is distinctive in the trust that is generally evident in the relations between the institutions and the Ministry, in the consensual pattern of policymaking and the extent to which ideas about contributing to the public good are shared between the academic community and the main political parties. Norway is also an affluent country where universities and colleges receive between 80 per cent and 90 per cent of their income from the state; marketization, as seen in the UK, is unknown. Most students go to their local or regional university and are less concerned about institutional hierarchies than in many other countries. Any significant reduction in resources might, however, have the effect of disturbing the balance of central and institutional governance controls now in place. Demographic changes, suggesting a realignment of the distribution of campuses might, for example, set real challenges between central authority and institutional autonomy where regional interests, ventilated at national levels, might spark conflict at an institutional level. In these circumstances, the underlying coherence of the system and the balance between central and institutional interests might find themselves coming under severe strain. Norway is a country committed to a policy of equalizing the economic and social interests of regions with those of metropolitan areas but also to a policy of university autonomy and self-governance. The proposal for Councils for Cooperation with Work Life, which itself was well intentioned, illustrates the limits of the powers of a centralized authority like a Ministry to implement a policy, conceived centrally, which impinged on institutional/regional inter relationships even when the broad policy issues are generally completely uncontroversial.

7.2 Regional policy and Ireland's technological universities: Balancing national and institutional ambition Ellen Hazelkorn

Introduction

This part of the chapter looks at the tensions between a highly centralized system of government in Ireland and limited devolution to sub-national levels through the lens of a growing focus on regional policy, and the intersection with higher education policy. It looks at the way in which regional policy has influenced the role and responsibilities of higher education institutions in Ireland, leading to the formation of technological universities. There are four sections: section one traces the ebbs and flows of regional policy, section two looks at changes in higher education policy; section three takes a closer look at the formation of technological universities, while section four concludes with observations on the links between and influence of regional policy and higher education.

The primary sub-national tier of government in Ireland operates at the level of the county – of which there are twenty-six – rather than the region; in addition, there are city councils for Dublin, Cork and Galway. Despite historic and emotive references to four provinces (Leinster, Connaught, Munster and Ulster), regionalism is not a strong concept. Ireland's centralized approach to policy- and decision-making is illustrated by the fact that the road and rail network operate as spokes from Dublin. Anyone travelling north to south or vice versa must do so by first travelling via Dublin. Colloquial language reinforces this notion; regardless of where one is geographically located vis-à-vis Dublin, people talk of 'going up to Dublin'. Despite this penchant for central government, one cannot override the much stronger social, cultural, sporting and political allegiance to county – albeit not region.

Over the decades, concerns have been expressed about urban/rural disparities arising from historic problems of emigration and rural poverty, an overconcentration of economic activity in the Dublin region, and a legacy of imbalanced infrastructure and contradictory social outcomes. Adoption of the knowledge economy paradigm in the late twentieth century led to the transformative economic upswing of the Celtic Tiger era – the term used to describe the boom years between 1995 and 2007. This was followed by the downturn of the global financial crisis and Great Recession only to be followed by another cycle of growth and then decline prompted by the Covid pandemic. Ireland's economic success is due to the strength of and overdependence on the international multinational sector. This makes Ireland – a small open economy, part of the EU but on the edge of Europe – particularly vulnerable to international economic trends. Brexit will create its own challenges.

The scale of population growth over recent decades and projected for the future is particularly noteworthy. Total population is estimated to rise from almost 3 million in 1956 to 5 million today to 6.7 million by 2051 due to natural increase, declining outward migration and rising inward migration (Central Statistical Office (CSO) 2018). Under current trends, agglomeration effects have elevated Dublin vis-à-vis other cities and towns across the country leading to challenges associated with urban sprawl and congestion with implications for people and families (Barrett 2018; Morgenroth 2008, 2018). The Greater Dublin region (Dublin and Mid-East) is projected to account for about 42 per cent of the total population and approximately 46.5 per cent of jobs by 2040. Regional disparity is evident also with respect to employment and unemployment levels with rural areas disproportionally affected (Bergin, Kelly and Redmond 2020).

Regional disparity has had a significant influence on student choice and hence participation rates over the decades with 'counties which are a distance from a university having a lower rate of admission to university education' (Clancy 1995: 160; Cullinan and Halpin 2017). Today, of the nine publicly funded universities, four are in Dublin. Forty-five per cent of students attend a Dublin-based institution, and 68 per cent of those who attended college in Dublin were working there nine months later. Of the 2018 graduating year, 46 per cent of honours degree graduates were working in Dublin with

12 per cent in Cork, 7 per cent in Galway and 6 per cent in Limerick. Of taught postgraduates, 50 per cent were working in Dublin and 13 per cent working in Cork with just 4 per cent finding employment in the southeast, 2 per cent in the border region and only 3 per cent in the midlands (Higher Education Authority (HEA) 2020).

Over the latter decades of the twentieth century, the big story has been massification; quite simply, for a country lacking natural resources, the aim has been to get more people well-educated. Society has been transformed from being a labour-exporting one to one heavily dependent upon highly skilled labour and skilled-immigration. It has also spurred significant expansion in national funding for research and science and technology-related matters, and greater focus on enterprise-academy collaboration. The landscape of Irish higher education has been transformed not just in the number and size of institutions but in their national role and international orientation. The Universities Act 1997 (Government of Ireland 1997: S12(f)) described university responsibility 'to support and contribute to the realisation of national economic and social development' while Institutes of Technology (IoT) were to 'provide vocational and technical education … with particular reference to the region served by the college' (Government of Ireland, Regional Technical Colleges Act 1992: S5(1)). Today, higher education – its graduates and research – are widely recognized as key to Ireland's economic progress.

These factors help to explain policy thinking about regions as well as for the reorganization of further education and training (FET) beginning 2013 and the merger of institutes of technology (IoT) and the formation of technological universities (TU) beginning 2018. Five technological universities – in Dublin, the southeast, southwest, mid-west, and northwest – will be established between 2020–2. It is anticipated they will play a dynamic role in their regions not least because two of the regions (southeast and northwest) have no university – a gap which has become a hot political issue and an economic imperative. Nonetheless, despite these developments, the concept of region remains both conceptually and politically weak in Ireland. The country retains a centrally dominated political system. Regionally based assemblies and county-based local government have limited authority and limited independent financial resources. They act primarily as executives of central government policy at local level. Regionalism is principally based on the idea of economic growth rather than having a multidimensional perspective. This is reflected in the fact that the NUTS classification system[2] bears little connection to a culturally and historically held sense of place.

Balancing national and regional policy

Irish independence ushered in a period of economic protectionism and self-sufficiency, underpinned by conservative Catholic nationalism beginning 1932. However, by the 1950s it was clear that policy had failed to kick-start an indigenous capitalist economy. Agriculture, the traditional mainstay of the Irish economy declined and little effort was given to developing new industries to fill the gap; net emigration peaked at 60,000 in 1957, roughly 2 per cent of the population (MacFeely 2016).

The First Programme for Economic Expansion (1958) set the scene for a dramatic *volte face*. Policy support for trade liberalization and incentives for foreign direct investment (FDI), initially with a strong focus on capital-intensive and then knowledge-intensive export-oriented production and services ensued. Ireland was viewed as a single economic entity with little effort being made to balance political decision-making or national and regional growth. While there was some discussion favouring decentralization, the overwhelming emphasis was on FDI with the country being perceived as a good location for low-skilled assembly. At the time, local industry was considered too weak to do much else.

Over the decades, different approaches to balancing national and regional challenges and ambitions have been proposed. Underpinning almost all big policy developments has been membership of the OECD – Ireland was a founding member in 1961 – and the European Economic Community – Ireland joined alongside the UK in 1973. Regional policy with an emphasis on economic development and social cohesion is no different, but it was not until the Telesis Report of 1982 (National Economic and Social Council (NESC), 1982), which starkly criticized the over-reliance on foreign multinationals, that government policy began, albeit slowly, to turn its attention to helping grow Irish-owned businesses around the country.

The Buchanan Report was published in 1968. It recommended moving away from an ad hoc dispersed approach whereby foreign companies set up wherever they thought best to a policy which targeted particular centres. Over the years, the idea of building on and building up a select set of towns around the country, in addition to Dublin, was presented in various versions. However, targeting select urban centres for growth was usually interpreted as ignoring or leaving rural Ireland behind and hence was hugely controversial. As a result, a conscious regional policy only began to emerge in the last decades. A National Spatial Strategy (NSS), 2002, was applauded for going beyond economic development to consider 'the wider set of factors driving regional development in a modern economy' (Morgenroth and Fitzgerald 2006: 76). It identified Dublin, Cork, Limerick, Galway and Waterford as national gateways while other towns were considered to be economic bridges between the larger cities and the rural hinterland.

Project Ireland 2040, launched in 2018, represents the most ambitious and comprehensive attempt at balanced regional growth (Government of Ireland 2018c). Along with the National Development Plan (Government of Ireland 2018a) and the National Planning Framework (Government of Ireland 2018b: 14), it again targeted specific cities and regional centres and towns for growth while recognizing Dublin's ongoing key role. Enhancing regional accessibility and strengthening rural economies and communities were named as 'shared goals – our national strategic outcomes'.

Efforts to establish regional structures have largely been shaped by 'pragmatic' responses to EU funding criteria (Quinn 2014). That 'regional policy ... was largely delegated to a 'top-down' industrial policy' was also an unintended consequence of designating Ireland as a single Objective 1 region upon entering the European Economic Community (MacFeely, 2016). The aim was to maximize the amount of funding Ireland received under EU Structural, Cohesion and Agricultural policies but did 'little to champion regional issues ... and the experimentation that occurred regarding regional policy was rigidly controlled by the centre' (Quinn 2014: 32). The EU smart specialization agenda is another example of this transactionally-led relationship between Ireland and the EU. After all, having a national or regional smart specialization strategy is an ex-ante conditionality of European Structural Funds.

Eight regional authorities linked to NUTS 3 regions were established in 1994. By 1999, economic growth was such that Ireland exceeded the guidelines and new arguments were promoted for splitting Ireland into two regions. In 2014, three regional assemblies linked to NUTS 2[3] designation were tasked with coordinating, promoting and supporting strategic and sustainable development in the regions (Government of Ireland 2018b).

From technical education to technological universities

In many respects, the Irish experience of post-secondary expansion is similar to elsewhere in Europe (Hazelkorn, Gibson and Harkin, 2015). At the start of the twentieth century, 3,200 students were enrolled at six universities on the island of Ireland. Today, there are almost 230,000 full- and part-time students enrolled across twenty-seven government-aided institutions in the Republic of Ireland, principally universities (traditional and technological) and institutes of technology (IoT) (Piggot 2020). In addition, there are approximately 27,000 students enrolled in the private higher education (PHE) sector.

The report of the Steering Committee on Technical Education (1967) urged the creation of regional technical colleges to meet the economic imperative for technically qualified people (Mulcahy et al. 1967), but it was not until the European Social Fund (ESF) began to provide the essential financial support in 1975 that expansion actually began (Barry, 2007). Between 1967 and 2000, thirteen regional technical colleges (RTC) were established to educate students 'for trade and industry over a broad spectrum of occupations ranging from craft to professional level, notably in engineering and science, but also in commercial, linguistic and other specialities' (Government of Ireland 1967; McMahon 2008). The role of colleges playing a 'developmental role in their region' was reflected in the regional distribution of the RTCs and their mission (Thorn 2018: 90).

Beginning in the 1980s, RTCs began to 'mirror government development policy' with an emphasis on emerging specialisms such as food science, polymers and chemical and marine engineering (Thorn 2018: 4). Educational provision gradually expanded from sub-degree (Level 6–7 on the national qualifications framework) to (honours) bachelors (Level 8) and then to masters and doctorate (Level 9 and 10). Their research and consultancy role was also strengthened (Hardiman et al. 1987: 39).

These developments reflected labour market pressures and increasing demand for application-oriented research associated with the expanding economy and the need to build up Irish enterprise (Hazelkorn and Moynihan

2010). Indeed, they contributed to an on-going discussion, prompted largely by the sector itself, about its future position and role in light of 'regional imperatives, global competitiveness, a new National Spatial Strategy and the process of creating a new European Higher Education Area' (CoD 2003: 8; CoD 1993; Skillbeck 2001). Following the establishment of the Dublin Institute of Technology (DIT) in 1992, all RTCs were renamed institutes of technology in recognition of their changing role(Duff, Hegarty, and Hussey, 2000). In 2007, all IoTs, including DIT, were brought under the remit of the Higher Education Authority (HEA).

In 2004, the OECD was asked to review the Irish higher education system. The review noted that while massification had been 'enormously beneficial both to Irish society and to the economy', the system now stood at a crossroads as it strives to meet the government's strategic objectives of 'placing its higher education system in the top ranks of OECD in terms of both quality and level of participation and creating a world class research, development and innovation capacity'. It recommended adoption of a strategic framework integrated with economic and regional policy whilst maintaining clear differentiation of roles between universities and IoTs within a binary system (OECD 2006).

The *National Strategy for Higher Education to 2030* (Higher Education Strategy Group 2011) built upon the OECD's recommendations. It supported strategic steering and shaping of the higher education landscape creating a coordinated and 'coherent' system of a smaller number of larger and diverse institutions, referred to as 'directed diversity' (Boland 2009). It also argued that publicly funded higher education institutions should respond more directly to national needs and accordingly should participate in regional clusters. It also advanced the theme of differentiation by proposing a 'process of consolidation that could potentially result in the redesignation of some institutes [of technology] as technological universities'. They would have distinct missions with new performance challenges (Higher Education Strategy Group 2011: 96, 102–3).

The National Strategy introduced new concepts, such as, collaboration and regional clusters into higher education thinking and policy-speak. All higher education institutions – universities and IoTs – were asked to be actively engaged 'with business and industry, with the civic life of the community, with public policy and practice, with artistic, cultural and sporting life and with other educational providers in the community and region', and involved in regionally based collaborations (Higher Education Strategy Group 2011: 74). Clusters were required to:

> determine and meet the needs of a wide range of students, communities and enterprises in their region. This will require joint programme planning, collaborative research and outreach initiatives, agreements on mutual recognition and progression, and joint strategies for advancing regional economic and social development. The institutions will also engage with other statutory providers of education and training, such as FÁS and the VECs, to develop integrated regional learning strategies. (Higher Education Strategy Group 2011: 98).

The HEA reinforced this message stating that while 'Mergers might or might not happen ... clusters must happen' (HEA 2011: 7) thereby illustrating the extent to which policy thinking was now firmly focused on collaboration and higher education 'as an economic asset' (HEA 2012, 2013).

Technological universities

For technological universities, regional characteristics and commitments are more than symbolic. The criteria for successful designation of technological universities was unequivocal in stressing that technological universities were to be mission distinctive (Hinfelaar 2012; Marginson 2012). In addition to emphasizing that they must continue their role with respect to widening participation and vocational/professional educational orientation, TUs should have 'particular regard to the needs of the region in which the university is located' (HEA 2012: 14; TU4Dublin 2013).

The Technological Universities Act 2018 (Government of Ireland 2018d: S9 (1)) describes the function of a technological university as 'having particular regard to the needs of the region in which the campuses of the technological university are located ...'. Regional relevance is mentioned repeatedly with regard to 'programmes of education and training', research and knowledge transfer and innovation 'arising from that research', collaboration with 'business, enterprise, the professions, the community, local interests and related stakeholders, supporting 'mobility of staff and students ... into and out of the labour force', serving the community, 'fostering close and effective relationships', and promoting access.

The process for designation as a technological university requires a consortia of two or more institutes of technology to come together with the intention of merging. In addition to meeting auditable baseline data with regards to student numbers and staff qualifications, S28 of the Act requires applicant IoTs to demonstrate they enrol students from the region, that its RDI activity 'has positive social and economic effects' on the region, that they have

> strong links with business, enterprise, the professions, the community, local interests and other stakeholders in the region

and that they have

> procedures in place to develop programmes that respond to the needs of business, enterprise, the professions, the community, local interests and other related stakeholders in the region.

The TU legislation is book-ended by the TURN Report, the outcome of a working group convened by the Department of Education and Skills and bringing together senior representatives from across the sector. With the strap line 'Connectedness and Collaboration through Connectivity', it set out the 'vision and ambition' for technological universities, and 'how it can be achieved'. It underscored the 'distinctive national and international contribution' of technological universities (TURN 2019). The regional dimension was also stitched into the strategic dialogue process that forms the basis for performance agreements between the Higher Education Authority and each HEI (Costello and Hazelkorn 2018).[4]

The regional role was further strengthened in Project Ireland 2040 Building Ireland's Future which name-checked technological universities. National Policy Objective 31 notes that

> By creating institutions of scale and strength, multi-campus technological universities will bring greater social and economic benefits to their regions through a strengthened role in research and innovation and the delivery of a broad range of high quality education and training in each of their campuses. (Government of Ireland, 2018b)

Special mention was given to TUs in Dublin, the south-east playing a key role in response to Brexit and the northwest along the economically weaker Atlantic Economic Corridor.

Provision of a formal pathway to (technological) university designation marked a landmark reshaping and consolidation of Irish higher education. At the time of writing, three technological universities have been designated following an international review (Technological University Dublin [TU Dublin] 2020;[5] Munster Technological University [MTU] 2021;[6] Technological University of the Shannon: Midlands Midwest 2021[7]) and two are likely to be designated starting early 2022 (South East Technological University [SETU] and Connaught Ulster).[8] Ironically given the regional importance, the international panels which conducted the reviews had no singular expertise in regional economic development.

The TURN Report is arguably the manual of technological universities. This reflects the fact that the nomenclature surrounding the TU was vague and had been adopted to ensure mission differentiation and hence to reassure critics. Otherwise, there was no real clarity about what TUs would do beyond simplistic references to *viz.* MIT, TU Munich or RWTH Aachen and/or to regional development. TURN made an important contribution by harvesting relevant policy and academic literature around higher education as an anchor institution and spelling out the implications for skills and human capital development, the digital economy and 'fuelling balanced regional development'. In doing so it provided the basis for multi-million Euro investment.

Linking regions and higher education

Since the 1990s, a strong and enduring feature of Irish economic and innovation policy has been the role of higher education and university-based research as a driver of skills and growth. Notably the 2014 Action Plan for Jobs included a commitment to 'Progress Enactment of the Technological University Bill' (Action 175) (Department of Jobs 2014: 52). The HEA played a key role in putting the concept of regions, place-based thinking and the formation of clusters of collaborating institutions on the map for higher education – although its enduring success has been setting the path for technological universities.[9] The HEA prompted early discussion around smart specialization in line with the EU discourse but this was not sustained. Given their history and geographic location, the TUs have a legacy commitment to vocational and professional education, and regional enterprise and innovation which is hardwired into the legislation. This is due in no small part to the fact that they have often been the only institution of higher education in their county. Nonetheless, TU commitment is too often more implicit than explicit and more superficial than deeply understood or articulated. Regional engagement is confused or subsumed within widening access, life-long learning or entrepreneurship activities rather than envisaged as a holistic regional or civic engagement agenda as widely understood elsewhere. This is evidenced by the absence of formal structures for on-going institutional-level engagement with external stakeholders or within the institutions themselves, relying instead on individualized actions.

Regionalism and regional policy has primarily been owned and driven by the enterprise-oriented departments. The smart specialization agenda was led by Science Foundation Ireland and the Department of Jobs, Enterprise and Innovation with a limited involvement of the higher education community. In reality, Ireland's smart specialization strategy was the research prioritization strategy under another guise (DJEI 2014: 16). Even the Department of Education and Skills favoured the more narrowly focused *Regional Skills Fora* (RSF)[10] rather than the more expansive regional clusters promoted by the HEA. RSF were established in 2016 as part of the National Skills Strategy to provide an opportunity for employers and the education and training system to work together to meet the emerging skills needs of their regions. By bringing further and higher education together, the RSF represented the first cross-sectoral structure, at a national and regional level, of note but there has been little spill-over effect on policy or institutional thinking.

Today, regionalism is increasingly part of the national policy discourse prompted by evidence that left unchecked Dublin would continue to draw in investment and population exposing growing national disparities. The most logical policy response would be to build-up a few cities as regional gateways, but local politics always intervenes. An alternative perspective proffers the advantages of Ireland's geographic size; measuring just 70,273 square km/27,132 square miles with an improving road network, no place is arguably further than three hours from Dublin by car. Project 2040 sought to bring together an array of different and competing policies and structures but there has been little shift in the balance of decision-making or public thinking around the issues. Despite regions having different socio-economic characteristics, policies and structures are similar. Plebiscites for changes in local governance arrangements, including the possibility of directly elected mayors in the larger cities, have met with varying levels of support. The HEA's role is limited to pursuance of TUs and the strategic dialogue process. There is little energy either behind deeper consideration of regionalism and the role of higher education in the Department of Further and Higher Education. In conclusion, while there is a lot of talk about regional policy, Ireland retains a very highly centralized system of governance.

7.3 Higher education and regional engagement in Germany *Jürgen Enders*

Introduction

This section discusses the development and current state of the regional engagement of higher education institutions in Germany. A special focus will be on the external and internal governance of the regional role and the contribution of higher education institutions. As regards the external governance of higher education institutions within the federal system, the prime responsibility for their regulation and funding resides with the sixteen *Länder*. This federal structure also influences the internal governance of higher education institutions for which significant differences can, at least formally, be found between the various *Länder*. The federal government may set some legal framework conditions, is heavily involved in infrastructural funding and research funding, and collaborates with the *Länder* in joint programmes and funding initiatives but in fact, and due to constitutional rules, the *Länder* and the federal government have to take care of joint coordination. This political architecture leads to a constant need for consultation, negotiation and political compromise among the various *Länder* and with the federal government.

In the following, an overview is provided first of the classical linkages of higher education institutions with their regions and related contributions to regional development. Related considerations by the *Länder* in respect of the positive side-effects of higher education institutions for their region played an important role in establishing new higher education institutions in the wake of the massification of higher education. Especially a new type of higher education institutions, the universities of applied science (*Fachhochschulen*), were expected to play more of a regional role than traditional universities.

Second, more recent trends in regional engagement and their governance are discussed: the arrival of regional contributions of higher education as one of the main topics in the political discourse on German higher education and science, including the potential for the universities of applied science to provide applied research and development to stimulate regional innovation and economic development; the prominent role of competitive short-term project-related funding programmes for regional engagement to incentivize bottom-up activities in institutions and stimulate partnerships, networks, and clusters of heterogeneous actors from higher education and science, business and civil society.

This section continues by discussing certain tensions and dilemmas in the governance of higher education-region interactions. It seeks to show that overall funding trends for higher education run counter to political measures that aim to incentivize higher education institutions to contribute to regional development. Further, the Bologna Process with its new Bachelors'-Masters' degree structure fosters regional student mobility and weakens chances of keeping students and graduates in structurally weaker regions across the country. Finally, the soft political approach towards regional engagement and the remarkable absence of strong political steering by the federal government or of coercive pressures from the *Länder* are discussed. The German approach relies heavily on the willingness and capacities of individual higher education institutions to engage with their regional role while we observe persistent heterogeneity in the internal governance and strategic orientations of higher education institutions as regards the cooperation with their region.

Finally, the conclusion summarizes the overall position of Germany in respect to higher education's regional engagement and its expected role in the future.

The development of the relationship between higher education and the region: An overview

In Germany, as in many other countries, universities have always had some role in their region just by being there. They contribute to the socio-economic standing and development of the region, for example, through investment in their infrastructure, the private spending of their staff and students, and by keeping students and graduates within the region or attracting students from other parts of the country to the region. In addition, universities, their staff and students also contribute to the cultural and political life of the region. Such positive impacts of universities on regional development and the effect of such linkages on regional employment and income are well known and continue to be important. A meta-study of forty-six publications outlines, for example, the breadth and magnitude of such regional economic effects of universities and other higher education providers (Drucker and Goldstein 2007). Valero and Van Reenen (2016) provide a related study about the positive economic effect of the establishment of new universities for seventy-eight countries. For Germany, a national study of such effects estimated that every Euro of public investment into higher education has multiplier effects in the regional economy that add up to more than one Euro (depending on the size of the higher education institution this effect is frequently in the order of between 1.4 and 1.6, Schubert and Kroll 2013). Recent studies have also shown how some German universities link up with their region to make them more environmentally friendly and sustainable (Radinger-Peer et al. 2019), and how the presence of such a university contributes to a political climate in which it becomes more likely that members of the Green party get elected to regional political leadership (Back and Fürst 2011).

In the wake of massification, universities' contributions to their regions became part and parcel of the considerations in public policies for the expansion of the sector as well as for the establishment of a new type of higher education institutions, the *Fachhochschulen*, called in more recent times the universities of applied science, that were expected to play more of a regional role than traditional universities. In Germany, some new universities and many new universities of applied science were in peripheral and/or structurally weaker regions (although almost every big city also hosts at least one). Higher education institutions in general and universities of applied science in particular thus became more of a political instrument for regional development (Fritsch 2009). The *Länder* identified the potential of newly established higher education institutions and especially the establishment of universities of applied science as smaller, more teaching oriented, and more regionally focused providers to support regional development: creating new employment in the region, functioning as potential catalysts of regional innovation by linking the educational offering more closely to the regional economy, and above all creating easily accessible educational opportunities for regional high school graduates including widening participation for young people from less well-off families. In addition, many structurally weaker regions were offered ample space and real estate; many campuses opened at abandoned military compounds or former industrial sites given up in the wake of economic restructurings so that public investment into higher education institutions did not have to compete with financially potent private investors, as would be more likely the case in metropolitan regions.

Regional interests and considerations also played a role in the establishment of new universities, as exemplified by two universities established in the wake of massification. One was located in the former industrial heartland of West Germany traditionally dominated by coal mining and steel working. Its foundation was intended as a political measure to counterbalance the decline of these industries and to provide graduates for infrastructural transformation towards a post-industrial economy. In addition, the university became the institution with the highest proportion of first-generation students in Germany due to the growing intake of first- and second-generation children of migrant workers living in the region. The important function of the university for social mobility in the region has been institutionalized by establishing the office of a Pro-Vice Rector for 'Societal Responsibility, Diversity, and Internationalization'. The other institution was established as a technical university in one of Germany's big cities in addition to the traditional multi-disciplinary university. The educational offering of the technical university in engineering, applied sciences, and management studies was targeted towards regional industries and the university also established strong research links with local industry and business which currently form the major research funders for the university. Last but not least, regional interests may also play a role in the establishment or transfer of public research centres and laboratories organized in the Max-Planck-Society, the Fraunhofer Society, the Leibnitz Community and others which play an important part in the publicly funded research system in Germany. Such centres are a source of investment and prestige for regions and cities and form preferred research partners for universities.

In 1990, when reunification took place, the main political actors imposed the political responsibilities and structural features of higher education unchanged on East Germany including the authorities and relationships between the federal government and the *Länder*, the binary higher education system differentiating the profile and role of universities and universities of applied science, and the prominent role of public research centres and laboratories. It took, however, until the late 1990s for a regional role of higher education institutions to become legally acknowledged via a new federal higher education framework act that defined technology transfer as at least part and parcel of the functions of higher education institutions (Hochschulrahmengesetzes 1998). Over the years, many *Länder* followed the federal government and included knowledge and technology transfer in their own legislation also acknowledging related activities as part of the academic conditions of service for members of staff. Some *Länder* went a step further and raised expectations that higher education institutions might include such activities in their strategic planning, their reporting systems and their evaluations. Most notably perhaps, new rules and expectations led across the country to the widespread establishment of institutional technology transfer centres that were expected to stimulate transfer to and collaboration with private industry. The few reviews of their activities and impacts provide, however, a mixed picture: such centres were the first institutionalized expression of a more pro-active role in higher education institutions in linking their research and knowledge base to regional actors and gave that function some visibility within the institution. At the same time, such centres tended to be under funded, understaffed, and missing the expertise and networks inside and outside the institutions to stimulate wide-spread and sustainable transfer activities. Krücken (2003) even argued that the technology transfer centres could be regarded as examples of 'decoupling' where universities show their flexibility by establishing new structures in response to political expectations while these new structures remain by and large decoupled from the institutional core functions.

Recent trends in regional engagement

Over the last twenty years, political attention and initiative has turned more and more towards regional development in general and the role of higher education institutions in the region. Various overall developments are characteristic for this period.

Regional embeddedness and higher education institutions' contribution to regional development have featured more prominently in numerous policy papers and institutional mission statements. Certainly, regional engagement had finally arrived as one of the main topics in the political discourse in German higher education and science. In this regard, the following statement of the German Rectors' Conference (*Hochschulrektorenkonferenz*) on the role of higher education institutions in Germany (referring to both traditional universities and universities of applied science) may serve as an example:

> Above all, in teaching, research and development, they are central counterparts and cooperation partners for regional businesses, associations and educational institutions that often depend vitally on the technological and social knowhow and capacities of the higher education institutions. Overall, higher education institutions unfold substantial social and economic effects especially in their regional context. (Hochschulrektorenkonferenz (HRK) 2016: 2f)

In 2018, the influential German Science Council (*Wissenschaftsrat*), which provides among other things advice to federal- and *Länder*-level policymaking, published its recommendations on regional cooperation between scientific institutions. It states that

> The regional cooperation between scientific and non-scientific actors has been characterized by a remarkable dynamic in the last few decades. … In many regions, partners from science, business and society have come together and are working on profiling them as a 'knowledge' or 'science region'. The regional environment of a scientific institution thus presents itself as an opportunity as well as a sphere of responsibility: in the region, scientific institutions can, on the one hand, look for possibilities and opportunities to increase their efficiency in different performance dimensions. On the other hand, scientific institutions perceive their role as contact persons for non-scientific actors and drivers of innovation in the region and thus contribute to the attractiveness and economic efficiency of their environment and location. (Wissenschaftsrat 2018: 3)

Policymakers, intermediary bodies, higher education institutions and other actors increasingly embraced the concept of the 'Third Mission' widening the perspective on the regional engagement of education and science beyond classical, narrower views on technology transfer or the supply of graduates to the region.

Second, the traditionally more pronounced role of the universities of applied science to target their educational offerings at the region found more political attention and support. In addition, political attention was drawn to the already existing capacities and perhaps more importantly future potentials of the universities of applied science in providing applied research and development stimulating regional innovation and prosperity. Many *Länder*, for example, included research and development at the universities of applied science in their higher education laws and thus into the politically supported mission of these institutions. The universities of applied science were also encouraged to incorporate applied research and development into their institutional mission statements and strategic development plans. The Science Council (2010) called for measures to counter-balance certain structural features of the universities of applied science (very high teaching loads for all lecturers; lack of academic staff and infrastructure for research; lack of administrative support for research) and to develop more equal opportunities for the universities of applied science in competing for research funding from the German Research Council. Such political initiatives should not be underestimated given that the universities of applied science were traditionally not assigned any research role at all and that their academic staff tended to undertake research outside of their formal conditions of service. The inclusion of a research function in the universities of applied science also reinforced their 'academic drift' that was already in progress due to the extension of their educational offerings in the Bologna Process to Bachelors' and Masters' degrees (instead of Bachelors' degrees only).

Third, the federal government and the *Länder* developed a new funding strategy for higher education and rolled out numerous dedicated funding programmes, including those addressing the regional engagement of higher education institutions. The overall political philosophy of this shift can be summarized by the following keywords: moving resources from basic funding to short term programme funding; offering funding in competitively organized schemes; incentivizing bottom-up activities by central funding; stimulating partnerships, networks and clusters of heterogeneous actors from higher education and science, business and civil society.

Such short term and competitive programmes include for example the funding measure 'Innovative Higher Education' that supports third mission activities to boost research-based knowledge transfer and innovation. It is aimed in particular at small and mid-size universities and universities of applied science. The programme is directed at higher education institutions which have already put in place a coherent strategy of interaction with businesses and society and have existing structures for and experience in idea, knowledge and technology transfer activities. Private corporations, educational and research institutions, and non-profit organizations and associations located in the region may submit joint applications with a university or university consortium. Up to 550 million Euros are provided for ten years; at least half of the funding will be provided to universities of applied sciences or consortia coordinated by a university of applied sciences. The programme 'Region Innovative' aims to support consortia, networks and clusters of business and industry, higher education institutions and public research centres, public authorities, and societal actors. It exclusively supports joint projects from existing collaborations in structurally weak regions which support the development of the business infrastructure and the regional labour market.

Since 2015, the federal government has run another programme that addresses the research function of the universities of applied science and its regional contributions. The programme aims at funding innovation partnerships between business and universities of applied science in research and development. The programme mainly addresses universities of applied science which have already developed a strong profile in applied research with high potential for knowledge transfer and regional innovation. The programme supports partnerships with regional business, especially SMEs, to facilitate sustainable partnerships and strong research collaborations with multiplier effects for regional innovation and development. Such partnerships mainly address research topics in engineering and technology, such as for example 'Multimodal analytics and intelligent sensors for the health industry', 'Mobility and Energy for Metropolitan Change' or the 'Innovation Centre for Wind Energy, System Integration, and Batteries'.

Most recently, public policy has also seen a re-birth of the idea of using the establishment of new higher education institutions for fostering the development of structurally weak regions within the country. About 40 per cent of the population lives in regions that are considered to be structurally weak, most notably all the regions within East Germany. The higher education development plan of the government of an East German *Land* provides an example of recent political actions to provide rough strategic guidelines for the regional role and engagement of all higher education institutions. It contains the following recent mission-related statement that assigns for the first time a major role to higher education institutions in the regional development of the *Land*:

> The higher education institutions build a location factor of high importance for the economic and societal development of [the *Land*]. ... Their importance as a regional economic factor for the rather structurally weak state is eminently large and estimated in a national study as ten per cent of the *Land*'s GDP. Against this backdrop, higher education institutions are assigned a prominent role in mastering the coming challenges of the state. (Landtag Mecklenburg-Vorpommern 2015: 19)

The federal government and the *Land* of Saxony have teamed up in an open call for ideas towards the establishment of two new large-scale research centres that are expected to be established in the former coalfield regions in Saxony. Each centre would receive public funding of up to €170 million per year, to span the full spectrum of activities from basic research to application, address major societal challenges and provide innovative approaches to cooperation between science and industry. Other *Länder*, like Bavaria, have followed this approach, aiming at the establishment of new branches of higher education institutions or research centres in structurally weak areas.

A different approach can be found in well-developed metropolitan regions which are increasingly branding themselves as 'science cities' or 'science regions'. Having visible and highly reputed universities and research centres is not only a matter of national pride but also of regional pride and competition, and a matter of regional branding including the branding of cities and regions as science cities or science regions.

The regionally engaged university: tensions and dilemmas

Certainly, a more proactive approach in shaping the relationship between higher education and the region has finally arrived on the political agenda but it is not without tensions and dilemmas. Overall, higher education and science policy have been dominated by more long-standing major trends that are not concerned with regional development as such while they have indirect and sometimes unintended consequences for the capacity of higher education institutions to contribute to their region (Postlep and Blume 2019).

Since the end of the 1990s, German higher education policy has seen a major shift away from basic funding towards public funding shaped by the leitmotiv of competition and excellence. During the last three decades, public funding of higher education institutions via grants and time limited programmes has tripled while in this period basic funding has only increased by 30 per cent. An unintended consequence of this development has been that big, comprehensive, research-intensive universities have been able to attract substantially more short-term project specific funding than other universities and especially more than the smaller, more teaching-oriented universities of applied science. Public research funding has in consequence moved towards structurally strong regions with a developed innovation-oriented infrastructure. It has also moved away from the universities of applied science who play a stronger role in regional development while they possess less capacity to successfully compete for research funding. This overall funding trend thus runs counter to other political measures and funding streams that aim to support more equal living conditions across the country and incentivize higher education institutions to contribute to regional development.

With the introduction of the Bachelor-Master structure in the Bologna Process an increase in student mobility and thus competition between higher education institutions for students was one of the politically desired outcomes. Traditionally, at the beginning of their studies German students preferred universities that were spatially close to their home region to higher education institutions that were more distant. Many students then also remained in their university region after graduation. In the past, institutions in structurally weaker regions had good prospects of initially being preferred by students in their catchment area when choosing a course; regions also benefitted from a regional binding effect after graduation. The switch to the Bachelor-Master model now creates a break in the dependency of the spatial path, as the students can decide during their studies to take up the Master's degree at another higher education institution and this decision may be made under less home-related considerations than the decision to apply for the Bachelor's degree. If this is the case, the chances of keeping students in the region for the long term deteriorate, especially for higher education institutions in rural areas, which initially gain their student potential from their own regions. Empirical evidence suggests that it is especially the more regionally oriented universities of applied science which are affected by this pattern of regional student mobility known as 'Bologna drain'.

The overall change in public funding portrayed above has gone along with a more specific focus in supporting institutional collaborations, clusters and networks of heterogenous partners. This approach can be observed across the board of various funding programmes including programmes that specifically support regional development. Such a programme philosophy has the advantage that local actors can organize themselves according to their needs and aims eventually capitalizing on existing networks. A policy that is oriented towards sustainable regional development and considers the third mission of the universities can learn that it is not only the traditional transfer services of the university that have a role in strengthening the regional innovation potential. The node and translation function of higher education institutions in knowledge networks also has demonstrable relevance for enabling collaboration with partners in geographical proximity that can also contribute to regional development beyond those targeted by regional transfer services.

The German political approach to incentivizing the regional engagement of higher education institutions thus has its merits. There is, however, a remarkable absence of strong political steering by the federal government or coercive pressures from the *Länder*. Federal policy aims at balanced development in all parts of the country. This includes the stimulation of weak regions as well as the targeted promotion of growth centres with hoped-for spill-over effects in the neighboring regions. However, the federal level is not well placed to deal with specific regional problem areas. In contrast to this, it is the task of *Land* politics to even out disparities, especially within the *Land*. The powers of the *Länder* as regards a detailed steering of higher education institutions are, however, limited. With the transition to increased contract management, the transition to output control was completed and limits the powers of the *Länder* for intervention. The interests of municipalities and municipal associations are certainly specifically regionally oriented and primarily serve to make the location more attractive. Regional political actors possess, however, neither the political authority nor the funding to steer higher education institutions. As a result, instruments of soft external governance have become dominant while the implementation strategies for political requirements must largely be worked out by the universities themselves.

In this respect, the institutional landscape in higher education is characterized by heterogeneity. It can perhaps best be mapped by a classification of four types as regards the internal governance and strategic orientations of higher education institutions (Kujath, Pasternack and Radinger-Peer 2019) in cooperation with their region:

- Some higher education institutions do not include a specific role for contributions to regional development in their mission statements given that their self-understanding is dominantly oriented towards their role as international players in the production of knowledge. Certainly, such higher education institutions contribute to the region due to their financial spending within the regional economy and they may further be linked due to the voluntary engagement of their staff and students. Third mission activities for and within the region do, however, not receive special and institution-wide support. This type exclusively comprises universities, especially those that figure prominently in international and national rankings, have been successful or aim at being successful in the German Excellence initiative.
- Another type comprises institutions which pay attention to the needs of the regional economy when it comes to the development and offer of their educational programmes that may in part be targeted to regional needs. Otherwise, their mission is – as in the first type – dominated by a self-understanding as knowledge producers in the international scientific community. This type also comprises exclusively universities which define their mission as 'research universities' with contributions to the regional labour market due to regionally targeted educational offerings.
- A further type comprises institutions which have incorporated third mission activities, such as knowledge and technology transfer or the development of spin-off companies, into their mission and support such activities within their governance model. They aim to make a visible contribution to the regional innovation system providing material and symbolic support for such activities. This type comprises some universities

as well as some especially research-active universities of applied science.
- Finally, some higher education institutions can be regarded as regionally engaged institutions which see themselves as central actors in regional development. They aim at actively influencing regional development as change agents. Their governance addresses regional development with a view on the overall profile, resources, and competences of the institution beyond the classical focus on knowledge and technology transfer. This type would be dominated by universities of applied science while some universities, especially new universities, might also be found in this type.

With this background, it is indicative that the German Science Council published a position paper on knowledge and technology transfer as a strategic task for higher education institutions (Wissenschaftsrat 2016). The paper calls for policymaking and higher education institutions to give technology transfer greater weight as a dimension of academic work in the strategies of academic institutions and improve the institutional processes which enable successful transfer activities to take place.

Conclusion

There is little doubt that the combined effect of the massification of German higher education and the lasting regional disparities especially between the west and the east of the country have encouraged a political search for mobilizing higher education and research for regional development. As in many other countries, the regional provision of higher education was strengthened by the establishment of a new type of higher education institutions, the *Fachhochschulen*, the universities of applied sciences. Subsequently, political attention also thought to strengthen the potential of the universities of applied science in providing applied research and development to stimulate regional innovation and economic development. In addition, the *Länder* and the federal government incentivize regional engagement of universities and universities of applied sciences via numerous initiatives and programmes fostering partnerships, networks, and clusters of actors from higher education and science, business and civil society. In turn, higher education institutions, especially those which were not giving priority to competing for research excellence, have begun to incorporate a regional role into their mission and strategic development plans or to strengthen their already existing activities and networks within their region. It can thus be argued that the regional role of higher education has clearly gained in political and institutional prominence even in the absence of a coordinated strong and coherent political approach towards the relationship between higher education and the region.

It seems likely that this trend will not only continue but will gain momentum. Structural policies addressing regional disparities across the country have clearly acquired political attention at the federal level as well as at the level of the *Länder*. Political actors will aim at integrating higher education policy and science policy in a stronger and more targeted way into their measures for structural developments in weaker regions. In turn, higher education institutions might be regarded as a critical factor and important actor at the heart of regional policies, in terms of their direct contributions to the region as well as in terms of their potential to work as focal points in regional networks and clusters. Such future directions will, however, not be without challenges for the integration of regional engagement into the very fabric of higher education: policy makers will need to find ways for more sustainable support of regional activities beyond short term programmatic funding, and higher education institutions will need to find ways to provide framework conditions to their decentral units and academic staff embracing regional engagement as an entire part of their portfolio.

UK higher education policymaking tends to be intensely UK-centric albeit with occasional glances towards Australia or the US. The cases of Norway, Ireland and Germany point to the fact that there are many parallel policy dilemmas much closer to home. A discussion of the lessons to be learned from these European comparators appears in Chapter 8.

Notes

1   We wish to express our appreciation for the assistance in the compilation of this account provided by Dr Mari Elkin of the Nordic Institute for Studies in Innovation, Research and Education. The interpretations and opinions, are the responsibility of the authors.

2   NUTS regions are part of the EU Nomenclature of Territorial Units for Statistics, which is instrumental in the delivery of the Structural Fund and other regional-based programming. http://ec.europa.eu/eurostat/web/nuts/overview
3   There are three NUTS 2 regions in Ireland:

- Eastern and Midland Region – comprises the county councils of Dún Laoghaire-Rathdown, Fingal, Kildare, Laois, Longford, Louth, Meath, Offaly, South Dublin, Westmeath and Wicklow and the city council of Dublin.
- Northern and Western Region – comprises the county councils of Cavan, Donegal, Leitrim, Galway, Mayo, Monaghan, Roscommon and Sligo and the city council of Galway.
- Southern Region – comprises the county councils of Carlow, Clare, Cork, Kerry, Kilkenny, Tipperary and Wexford, the city council of Cork, and the city and county councils of Limerick and Waterford.

4   https://hea.ie/funding-governance-performance/managing-performance/system-performance-framework/
5   https://www.education.ie/en/Press-Events/Press-Releases/2019-press-releases/PR19-01-01.html
6   https://www.education.ie/en/Press-Events/Press-Releases/2020-press-releases/PR20-05-26.html
7   https://www.gov.ie/en/press-release/cf73e-minister-harris-confirms-establishment-of-technological-university-of-the-shannon-midlands-and-midwest/
8   Two IoTs remain. The Institute of Art, Design and Technology (IADT), and the Dundalk Institute of Technology.
9   https://hea.ie/policy/he-reform/technological-universities/

Chapter 8

Tertiary Education and the Role of Regions: The Case for Decentralization

The transfer from higher to tertiary education

Our research evidence has convinced us that the development of higher education and considerable social and economic benefits would be achieved by moving to a tertiary education system as has been adopted in Wales. Our findings in Chapter 4 confirm that intersectoral links between further and higher education are well developed in the UK, that further education colleges have a reach into communities which universities of their nature and structure cannot equal and that their role in providing encouragement in progression and self-belief to students unwilling or unable to leave their locality can be of critical importance to economically and socially deprived areas. From a 'levelling up' perspective a tertiary system, coordinated at regional level close to the point of activity, would mark a big step towards the better articulation of technical and technological education, the health sciences and other professions and in building back social capital into communities. Such a move would have implications for the present centralized machinery governing the two sectors. A centralized structure could not carry the weight of a sectoral merger unless it created its own regional machinery but that would have the potential effect of re-creating a centralized, top down, approach to policymaking, stifling local initiative and directly conflicting with a key tenet of the Levelling Up White Paper which was to emphasize the importance of a 'local growth policy' (Levelling Up White Paper 2022: para 1.7.2) and emphasizing local decision-making.

In practice, the nature of post-secondary education in two of our comparator country systems, Norway and Ireland, is tertiary with the universities of applied science, the university colleges and the universities of technology all having a considerable stake in non-degree education programmes which parallel provision in further education in the UK. In Germany a pre-1992 UK-style informal binary line still exists between traditional universities and *Fachhochschulen*, universities of applied science, which span non-degree, first degree and master's programmes. This is being eroded over time as the title of university of applied science promotes the *Fachhochschulens*' academic standing, as collaboration grows with universities and where *Länder* governments themselves choose to exercise greater coordination between the two sets of institutions. In that restricted sense, Germany offers a more useful model to England than Ireland or Norway, countries with small populations not too dissimilar in size to Scotland and Wales, where a centralization of policy and structural management may be appropriate to the size of the systems. We believe, however, that the evidence points to a transfer to a tertiary education system in England and is an essential element in any levelling up process.

Lessons from European comparators

Any discussion of the organizational implications of a move to a tertiary system takes us much closer to a central policy issue, the effectiveness of a centralized or decentralized approach to managing post-secondary education. We selected the Norwegian, Irish and German higher education systems because of the contrasts they offer both in comparison with the UK and in comparison with one another and the way they illustrate different approaches to issues of centralization and decentralization and the role of regions in the governance of their higher education structures. While Norway and Ireland remain heavily centralized in their systems, albeit with some important qualifications, Germany operates a regionally devolved governance system which, however, is significantly moderated by the federal government; in the UK a mixed picture has emerged with devolved systems having been initiated in Scotland, Wales and Northern Ireland, but with England by far the largest component of UK higher education remaining a highly centralized system. In Germany and Norway, the systems are underpinned by explicit commitments to the maintenance of economic and social equity between regions: in Germany legislation imposes a requirement for equality in living conditions across the different *Länder*, and in Norway there is an embedded political commitment to maintain equal access to higher education across every region. In the UK, no such commitment exists and the inequalities that exist between regions are conceded by the Levelling Up White Paper, following McCann, as being amongst the most extreme in Europe. In Ireland, Ellen Hazelkorn describes a situation where regional structures abound but in practice carry little balancing influence with a strongly centralized governing structure based in Dublin. It seems that redressing regional economic and social imbalances will be vested in the establishment of a new category of technological universities created out of mergers of regionally based institutes of technology rather than being coordinated region by region in the regional structures themselves. In Germany, Jurgen Enders shows how even with a regionally based political structure and in spite of an active discussion at national level about the role of higher education institutions vis à vis regions the historic distinctions between universities and *Fachhochschulen* apportion the regional role primarily to the latter, leaving the universities free to concentrate on their traditional research activities geared primarily to national agendas. In Norway, where regionalism is embedded in the political system and where great steps have been taken to address regional institutional issues it has still been the case that universities, new and old , have felt able to resist pressures from central government to establish regionally representative machinery for Cooperation with Work Life within institutions to drive regionally orientated academic work. Thus, none of these approaches achieve wholly satisfactory solution

In all these systems history and geophysical factors have played a significant part in determining patterns of centralization or decentralization. In Ireland, the centralization of civic, economic and cultural life in Dublin has strong historical roots heavily reinforced by its dominant position in the nineteenth century where the headquarters of the National University of Ireland was located. As Hazelkorn points out, it remains the central hub for travel between the north and the south of the Republic. However, until 1989, when the National Institutes of Higher Education in Dublin and Limerick were upgraded to university status as Dublin City University and the University of Limerick, the university system was confined to the former university colleges of the National University, in Cork, Dublin and Galway, founded in the nineteenth century together with Trinity College, Dublin founded in the seventeenth.

Similarly, Norway was dependent on long established universities in Bergen, Oslo and Trondheim, with Tromsø founded in 1972, and with government centred in Oslo. Both countries maintained 'elite', geographically unbalanced, traditionally centralized, systems until the 1990s. Germany, on the other hand, had a historically devolved state system, which was reinforced in 1946, together with a regionally spread range of universities since well before the First World War; its government never assumed the central policy reins in the same way as in Ireland and Norway. It did not in fact seek to establish an 'elite' system of universities comparable to the historically identified groups in Ireland and Norway until the introduction of the German Excellence Initiative in 2006.

By comparison, the UK centralized policymaking and management of the university system immediately after the First World War in 1919 with the creation of a University Grants Committee to coordinate state funding support to the universities. As student numbers grew in the post-Second World War expansion it created new universities patterned on the existing models. Regional considerations were only occasionally referenced in central decision-making until 1992 when the government, primarily for political and administrative reasons, having abolished the University Grants Committee, created separate Higher Education Funding Councils for England, Scotland and Wales. In 1998, policy on higher education was formally devolved along with a broad range of political, legislative and administrative power to Scotland and Wales, with Northern Ireland following in 1999.

The transfer from elite to mass to universal higher education (Trow 1974), and its implications for economic progress, vocational education and system finance have internationally forced the hands of political decision-makers to adapt their university-based systems to the new demands: regions and regionalism entered policy discussion in a way that challenged the traditional structures of university systems. Moreover, as the expansion of student numbers affected non-university institutions it fuelled aspirations for university status and the greater autonomy which this traditionally conferred; it also encouraged a rear-guard action in favour of long-established university structures, the maintenance of the research character deemed appropriate to university institutions and the place of the academic community in institutional governance.

Germany and the UK were the first to react to pressures for change though from different standpoints: in 1970, in a move designed in great part to protect the traditional idea of a university, Germany created a new category of institution, the *Fachhochschulen*, which were designedly vocational in mission, taught at degree equivalent and non-degree levels, but were not permitted to award doctorates and were not intended to be research-active. Most importantly, however, they were strongly orientated to a regional mission and were firmly under *Länder* control.

Three years earlier the UK had established a new range of institutions, the polytechnics (Scottish Central Institutions in Scotland) aimed at a broader spectrum of students than the traditional universities, both degree and non-degree, part-time and full-time, and answerable to local civic authorities not to a central government body. Unlike the *Fachhochschulen*, however, they were permitted to award doctorates after academic review through a central body, the Council for National Academic Awards (CNAA) which also validated their undergraduate degrees expressly on the basis of parity with existing university degrees. Again, but unlike the *Fachhochschulen*, they were not constrained to be vocational or to be regionally orientated and in practice, although their origins were in technical education, they also developed broadly-based curricula in the humanities and social sciences. However, like the *Fachhochschulen*, they were condemned to second tier status within the UK higher education system (or third tier if one took account of the findings of the UGC-organized research assessment exercises) and were not funded for research. By the early 1980s their student numbers – recruitment was effectively open-ended – exceeded those in the university sector where numbers had been constrained by government decision. In 1988, they were transferred from local authority to central control and in 1992 they were granted full university status with the same rights and freedoms as the existing universities. In the two decades following 2000, a further group of colleges has been upgraded, the so-called post-post-1992 universities, mostly former teacher training colleges. These colleges have had to go through a process of quality assessment by the Quality Assurance Agency (QAA) before being granted a change of status but have otherwise had no more restrictions on their freedom to develop their own mission than the polytechnics had before them. To complete the picture, in 1992 the further education colleges were also transferred from local authority to central control. The direction of travel was determinedly towards centralization.

The progress of transition in Ireland and Norway offers many sharp contrasts with Germany and the UK. The strategies of both have been explicitly aimed at correcting regional disparities, in each case seeking to rectify the anomalies arising from their histories, the concentration of universities in coastal ports in the south in the case of Norway and the dominance of Dublin in the case of Ireland. In Norway, the first task was to rationalize an extended college structure into larger organizations but in 2003 it deepened the process with the Quality Reform legislation which adopted the key principles of addressing the inequalities of access to higher education and strengthening the institutions themselves by reducing fragmentation through mergers. Similarly, in Ireland the solution to regional inequalities has been seen in merging the former institutes of technology to become universities of technology. In both cases, the mergers are designed to preserve the various institutional campuses and to envisage new merged institutions being created, pooling resources, but extending the institutions over widely distributed areas, very different to the concentration of facilities in the single locations of the previous generation of universities. In the implementation of these policies, both systems faced issues of internal comparability. Norway, with its Humboldtian origins, committed itself to restricting the award of university title to institutions engaged in research and laid down criteria to be evaluated by a newly established agency NOKUT to determine the categorization of institutions as universities, universities of applied science or university colleges. In practice, this allowed some institutions based on college mergers to move through a university of applied science stage to full university status. It also entrenched an atmosphere of academic drift where colleges could prioritize potential upward movement into university of applied science status over regional commitment. One result has been a weakening of the role of the Ministry and a transfer of powers to shape the system to NOKUT. Deciding to link university status to a Humboldtian research culture and its associated tradition of institutional autonomy has, however, imposed a political limitation on the state's freedom to manage the higher education system in spite of the fact that it provides between 80 to 90 per cent of its funding. The fate of the proposal for Councils of Cooperation with Work Life may offer an illustration of problems to come. In Ireland, the Higher Education Authority (HEA) has maintained a firmer control over merger proposals, and it is difficult to believe that the new universities of technology will not remain a distinctly separate sector in the Irish university system rather than achieve full parity of esteem with the traditional universities. Here the parallel must be with Germany where the *Fachhochschulen* have now also assumed university, albeit of applied science, status and some are even engaged jointly with comprehensive universities to share doctoral teaching. The introduction of master's programmes following the Bologna Process has, as Jurgen Enders shows, increased the possibility of academic drift.

Thus, in all our European comparators we find that regionalism has played a critical role in the transformation from elite to mass higher education. In Norway, it has driven first the restructuring of the college sector, second the opening up of the university sector to new entrants, and third it has massively contributed to widening participation. In Ireland, it has refocused the institutes of technology into key regional actors as universities of technology. In Germany, while it has preserved a perhaps conservative perspective on the university system's mission (although Jurgen Enders makes it clear that many universities do in fact play regional roles of their own volition) it has incentivized the *Fachhochschulen* by permitting them the title of university of applied science and, through funding, to play important regional roles both in technical education and in applied research. However, in the UK we find little evidence in the past of a recognition of higher education having a regional role. While regional factors played only a minimal part in decisions on the siting of new universities in the 1960s and early 1970s, no consideration at all appears to have been given in 1988 when the polytechnics were transferred from local authority to central government control to the idea that this might be an opportunity to encourage an explicitly regional mission and, in 1992, the unthinking assumption of institutional upgrading was simply that it would create another tier in an enlarged university system and stimulate competition with the existing university sector. The decision to decentralize and then to devolve the management of higher education to Scotland, Wales and Northern Ireland (while retaining a central UK spending power and strategic control over research policy) was not taken in relation either to policy issues in higher education or to the role universities might play in the new devolved regions. The decisions in England to upgrade a number of higher education colleges in the years after 2000 may have reflected a view as to the economic benefits to the locality of enhanced institutional expenditure but was not accompanied by any formal encouragement to orient academic work towards regional development. A Higher Education Innovation Fund (HEIF) was aimed to encourage work in the wider economic community but was not specifically regionally directed; both the Department for Education and the Department for Business, Innovation and Skills (and its successors) may be described as tone-deaf where universities and regional policies are concerned.

What is clear from the three country accounts is that managing the process of elite to mass and to universal higher education is fraught with difficulties for all countries and is framed by legislative, constitutional and historical traditions which to a large extent determine solutions. In Ireland and Norway, the task has been to spread the opportunities for higher education outwards from metropolitan centres to provincial/rural hinterlands; in Germany it has been to incentivize the *Fachhochschulen* to take on extended regional roles. In Germany and in Norway, the long-standing political (and in the German case, constitutional) requirement to pursue policies which engendered equality between regions have provided the focus to drive the developments. No such focus exists in England although there is general public acceptance of the need for 'levelling up' regional inequality. The practical and policy issues are that much more formidable; higher education policy in England has been largely devoted to issues surrounding tuition fees and research; it has failed to recognize its relationship to regional issues.

The case for the decentralization of higher education in England

One advantage of the UK situation is that some decentralization has already taken place in respect to Scotland, Wales and Northern Ireland, and it is possible to make judgements on its effectiveness and the benefits it has brought. We made a detailed assessment of the impact on the higher education systems of the three nations in *The Governance of British Higher Education: The impact of governmental, financial and market pressures* (Shattock and Horvath 2019: Ch. 2) and in Shattock and Horvath 2020. We found that the process had been almost entirely positive in Scotland and Wales, but we concluded that the political and social situation in Northern Ireland had had the effect of blocking the possibility of developments based on local initiative. The Northern Ireland situation, in fact, flagged up an important caveat to the success of regional decentralization in general because it emphasized the importance of appropriate governance structures at the regional level that would enable the benefits of decentralization to be realized. The key benefits obtained in Scotland and Wales may be summarized as follows:

- the distinctiveness of the system becomes more aligned to the characteristics (history, geopolitical landscape, economy and culture) within its region. An example in Scotland would be the decision to reject the payment of tuition fees as a basis for funding as being contrary to Scottish university tradition;
- the ability to shape, or re-shape, the effectiveness of the system to match shifts in demography, industrial decline or other local requirements on the basis of regional knowledge and perspective. An example in Wales would be the rationalization that has taken place of further education institutions;
- the encouragement of greater coherence and collaboration between groups of institutions including joint activities aimed at regenerating disadvantaged communities;
- the prospect of better integration of higher education institutions with regional economic and social planning enabling targeted regional investment to be more effective than centrally devised and directed regeneration programmes;
- the bringing together of institutions in their regions to create more coherent sets of opportunities for locally-based students and to encourage greater collaboration in research. An example in Scotland would be the Forth Valley project in which Stirling University is partnered with Forth Valley College, local authorities and schools in the Stirling and Clackmannanshire Town Fund project (albeit the actual funding for the project comes from the UK wide Town Fund programme).

It is difficult to see why the benefits outlined would not be realized in comparably sized regions in England.

A key step would be the removal of artificial bureaucratic boundaries between the two sectors. A first stage in such a process is exemplified in the London

Higher Civic Map which records the engagement of London's higher education institutions with their communities. London Higher, the umbrella body representing some forty or so institutions, describes the Map as 'celebrating the many ways in which London's higher education institutions work on and indeed beyond the traditional 'campus' for example engaging with the capital's business or partnering with health providers to benefit local communities and make a positive difference to society (London Higher 2021). Similar moves are taking place in the Sheffield City Regional Post-18 Education Partnership and in a Greater Manchester partnership (Morgan 2021). Removing the administrative divisions between higher and further education will accelerate the drive to decentralization. Decentralization would be administratively complex to put in place but is not in itself revolutionary (and is not to be confused with the process of wider government devolution as pursued in Scotland, Wales and Northern Ireland): there is a world-wide trend to decentralize governmental functions (Garmendia 2021; Hooghe and Marks 2016; Ladner et al. 2019; Loughlin et al. 2011; Schakel 2021) from which England has excluded itself and indeed is a laggard within Europe. Schakel provides an illuminating chart showing how the UK compares internationally in the way in which decentralization is distributed between local and regional governments (Schakel 2021: Fig. 3.3). The creation of Combined Authorities and 'metro-mayors', where municipal authorities have come together to establish common leadership and machinery to take on board powers devolved from central government offer a structure with which the decentralization of higher and further education might be integrated. It is clear that where they are in full operation, they are making an economic impact and reviving the concept of regional strategies; Giovannini finds that metro-mayors have been at the forefront 'of opening up new opportunities' (Giovannini 2021). They are the natural bodies to coordinate tertiary education systems with the economic and social strategies for their regions.

Schakel suggests that decentralization as a reform of central governance is driven by two main logics, functional logic and identity logic (Schakel 2021: 40). In the UK's case, devolution to Scotland and Wales (though not Northern Ireland) falls clearly into the second category, though our research would suggest that in all three cases considerable functionality also existed. We would argue that functional logic is the strongest driver of decentralization in higher and further education although in some parts of the country identity logic would certainly play a part (London, the North West and perhaps the South West). At its simplest what would be involved would be the merger of two currently centralized activities, higher education and further education, to form a common system with the decentralization of their control and development to regional authorities many of which are broadly comparable in population size to Wales, which has already adopted this pattern and demonstrated its success. Such thinking would, in principle, be in line with the White Paper's statement that 'the UK's centralized governance model means local actors have too rarely been empowered to design and deliver policies necessary for growth' (Levelling Up White Paper 2022: para 2.2.2) and its promise that the Government's new policy regime will include reshaping central government decision-making and emphasize local decision-taking (Levelling Up White Paper 2022: para 2.2.3).

Decentralization would need to embody some important principles:

- The first must be a clear decision on the level to which decentralization is pursued. In Germany, we have seen that while the *Länder* have controlling authority the interrelation of federal and *Länder* powers and the tradition of cross-national dialogue constrains regional governments from acting outside an agreed national framework. Tselios, writing about the decentralization of government functions in general, argues that partial decentralization rather than full decentralization may be the most effective option, and makes a statement that is of relevance to the case of English tertiary education: 'the optimal and effective co-participation of national and sub-national government in policy-making might be the best instrument to respond to income inequality' (Tselios 2021: 274). This principle could be said to be observed in the present UK devolution arrangements in that policy and funding in respect to research, including the operation of the research councils and the Research Excellence Framework (REF), remains reserved to central government in a non-departmental body, United Kingdom Research and Innovation (UKRI). While the mode of distribution of REF monies has been contested in Scotland there is no serious objection to control of the UK higher education research budget remaining a central responsibility, with Research England, a subsidiary of UKRI, managing the REF; this should be retained as part of the necessary balance between central and regional administration and as a long-term protection to the university system. Outside this element of centralization it is essential that the regional bodies have real powers and funding support to steer the new regional systems.

- A second principle should be the retention of a national Quality Assurance Agency (QAA) to maintain the common standing of the UK first and postgraduate degrees across the regions (also to give confidence to international student markets) and to offer independent guidance to central and regional authorities as appropriate as circumstances affecting individual institutions may seem to require it. Quality assurance should be by peer review, not metric-based, to ensure that communication about best practice and innovatory new approaches is spread across the regions.

- Governance and accountability: it would be important that regional authorities established representative committees which had devolved responsibilities for the management and development of tertiary education within their region. Their membership should be widely drawn from industry, the professions and from education, including the national academic community, and should not be local authority dominated. Some cross-representation with a LEP might be advantageous. Such committees should have legally prescribed powers and functions and should be accountable to their regional authority and to the secretary of state for education. Powers relating to the management of institutions currently vested in the Office for Students should be devolved to them but the Office itself would need to continue in a residual coordinating and regulatory role. National policy announcements, however, should be made direct to the chairs of the regional tertiary education committees as well as to institutional heads. Institutions should continue to be financially accountable to central government, as well as to their regional representative bodies but external audit arrangements should be undertaken by a joint national and regional audit organization. It would not be necessary or desirable to replicate the close interlocking of federal and *Länder* consultations apparent in the German system but there would be value in cross-regional communication between regional tertiary committees to compare good practice, in particular in respect to relationships with economic development or widening participation.

National services like the Higher Education Statistics Agency (HESA) and the Joint Information Systems Committee (Jisc) would not be affected.
- Funding: it would be important that the regional committees had access to those funds nationally allocated to the two sectors divided appropriately *pro rata* on their historic bases. In a situation where recurrent costs in English higher education are largely met from tuition fees this does not amount to very much. In the period 1998 to 2010, universities benefited from capital or project-based funds granted by the nine Regional Development Agencies (RDAs) in England. Their role has in part been taken over by the thirty-eight Local Enterprise Partnerships (LEPs). If the decentralization of a tertiary system is to be effective ways need to be found to provide these new regional tertiary education bodies with funding, whether an additional funding stream or by creating access to bodies like the LEPs, so that they can invest in new projects which link education to economic and social development in areas of deprivation whether it is to support extending the work of further education colleges into new low-participation areas, pump-priming new cross-institutional programmes to support regional industry or creating SME networks in new technological fields. If regional internal inequalities and the needs of disadvantaged communities are to be addressed through education and training, they need regionally-based funding arrangements on which they can draw to make regionally-based investments and the hands of the institutional dial need to point to regional sources for support rather than to funding streams defined and administered nationally.

A programme like this of the decentralization of decision-making need not be deferred while larger questions of the devolution of governance plans to regions are considered. A regional framework of Combined Authorities is in the process of being established with nine such regions now in existence. English higher education and its governance authorities now have the opportunity to establish a modern, effective decentralized system underpinned by a necessary central strategy for research which offers greater clarity and less blurring of boundaries, a better balance between regional and central government policies and a more purposive move to greater regional equality than any of the European comparators we have drawn on in this study. Consideration could now be given to enable the existing Combined Authorities to take over the implied responsibilities of a decentralized higher and further education system – no one can doubt the ability of Greater Manchester, the West Midlands and let alone London, to quote three large authorities, to take them on. It is not necessary to wait for a complete set of Combined Authorities to come into existence, as with the progress of the Combined Authorities' creation itself, for a decentralization of higher and further education to proceed. We hope that by outlining some ideas we shall have accelerated the process.

University autonomy in a decentralized system

Prominent among the doubters as to the value of decentralization are likely to be many of the universities themselves. Their two main arguments might be first, an apparent loss of status in their detachment from central decision-making and second, the danger that parochialism or regional politics, or simply non-academic priorities, would become paramount factors in decentralized decision-making. The record of local authority decision-making when in control of the polytechnics represents a lasting disincentive to encouraging any devolution of authority from the centre.

There is no evidence in other decentralized systems that these arguments are likely to be substantiated. In Germany, a country with a long history of decentralization, the respect for university autonomy and academic freedoms represents a key element in the balance of authority between the federal government, the *Länder* and the institutions to the extent that until now responsibility for the 'heavy lifting' of vocationalism and regional engagement has been consigned to the *Fachhochschule*n, the universities of applied science. In Norway, where the political support for regional policymaking is exceptionally strong, the Quality Reform programme gave colleges the freedom to make their own decisions about who to merge with and created NOKUT, an academically-orientated body, to make judgements on upgrading institutions and, in effect, shaping the system. Stensaker, who has written the definitive account of the transformation of the governance of the Norwegian system, entitled his account, ironically, as *Troublesome Institutional Autonomy: Governance and the distribution of authority in Norwegian universities* and noted that institutional autonomy 'had triggered a significant exposure to academic drift' and that 'very few institutions are actually undergoing a radical transformation to become more strategic actors' (Stensaker 2014). The inference to be drawn from these conclusions is amply borne out in the narrative about the requirement imposed on institutions to create Councils for Cooperation with Work Life. Although, as the account of the regional factor in Norwegian higher education, above, makes clear, the requirement came at a difficult time administratively for many institutions, the fact remains that most institutions seem to have disregarded it either as not contributing anything additional to their own strategies or because it suggested a competing piece of governance machinery for making strategy to what they already had in place. In other words, even in a country where the national priority for greater regional engagement was clear, institutional autonomy and the internal processes of self-governance asserted themselves. (It is too early in the life of the new universities of technology in Ireland to assess the extent of their autonomy as compared to the earlier generation of universities but the fact that Ireland has an intermediary body, the HEA, suggests that their autonomy will be protected.)

Closer to home, the evidence from thirty years of decentralization and devolution to Scotland and Wales does not suggest any weakening of institutional autonomy though it does suggest some change in relationships between the universities and the governments. In both countries universities benefit from face-to-face intimate meetings with Ministers (Shattock and Horvath 2019: 47 and 57) and from the government's familiarity with local contextual issues in a way that is inconceivable in England where there is a much larger number of institutions operating in a marketized system. In practice, the Welsh consensual approach to policymaking is much closer to the Norwegian model; in Scotland, relations with the Scottish National Party (SNP) government, where funding and the threat of government intervention arising from the requirement for institutions to complete Outcome Agreements represent significant issues, can be less congenial. In Scotland, too, the legislative imposition of changes to the make-up and operation of university governing bodies in 2016 showed how breakdowns can occur in areas where political interest is able to override institutional objections (Shattock and Horvath 2019: 56). On the other hand, such cases may also occur, and with more damaging generalized application in centralized systems. What we found in

Scotland and Wales was that universities obtained more and quicker access to a political process in decentralized structures than they ever did before. (In Northern Ireland, the absence of a proper political process emphasized the point made above that decentralizing authority over higher education authorities to regions requires that good governance of the institutions is protected through legislation, appropriate constitutional definition and legally defined powers of authority.)

Within higher education there might be particular concern about decentralization amongst research intensive universities where fears might exist that regional committees might give their claims for support a lower priority than those coming from universities with apparently more explicit regional missions. However, the success of the Universities of Edinburgh, Glasgow and Cardiff under thirty years of devolution suggests on the contrary that their high profile internationally and their enhanced political connections have considerably benefitted them. The close economic partnerships between the Universities of Leeds, Newcastle and Manchester and their respective civic and regional authorities described in Chapters 2 and 3 provides good evidence of the recognition of the importance of research reputation in a knowledge economy to cities and regions competing for industrial development or international investment. The fact that research and research policy would continue to be funded through UKRI and Research England would also provide a safeguard against radical policy realignment at the regional level.

There is no reason why the process of decentralization should lead to any diminution of institutional autonomy – it certainly has not in Germany – and in many ways it could enhance it in England if only by the introduction of a less bureaucratic, more institution-centric governance regime that was more obviously responsive to local and regional contexts. The evidence presented in Chapters 3, 4 and 5 provide testimony to the energy, enterprise and imagination with which our case study universities have pursued regional engagement in its many forms. Our belief is that these characteristics are constrained by a centralized decision-making system which is unable to take into account wide disparities in regional circumstances and by regulations and modes of governance which discourage diversity of mission and the pursuit of innovative solutions to local and regional problems. Most importantly decentralization would restore a policy input from regions as against the present bureaucracy of centralization, offer the prospect of a better articulation of the contribution that higher education institutions can make to regional planning and would provide greater prospects for local enterprise and innovation.

Decentralization would change the nature of central government's relationship with higher education in that it would become more a coordinator of regionally-based enterprises than the instigator of interventions arising from national political debate. Policy formation would be more bottom-up than top-down, but it would not remove the role of the centre from retaining a necessary regulatory function or from policymaking based on national concerns. The existence of the higher and further education representative bodies, Universities UK (UUK) and its mission groups and the Association of Colleges (AoC) would remain unchanged though their modes of operation would need to adapt to the new regional structures. Collaboration between UUK and any regional representative body that emerged would create a powerful pressure group for the interests of a tertiary system.

Further education in a tertiary setting

Further education has been described as the Cinderella service for as long as anyone can remember, its funding and *raison d'etre* falling between the two major components of the education system. In England there is little or any central policy coordination between the interests of further and higher education although, as the data in Chapter 4 indicates, over 80% of colleges and over 50 per cent of universities have developed formal programmatic links with one another. A transfer to a tertiary education system in which the policy and administration of the two sectors would be developed together would offer an end to the sectoral isolation of further education and its full integration with a wider arc of post-secondary policymaking, as well as, with decentralization , encouraging a closer and more direct engagement with local and regional needs. Its unique contribution to bridging the interface between secondary and post-secondary education and its relationship with social and economic disadvantage and the labour market could be fully realized.

However, a review of the Education and Skills Funding Agency (ESFA), conducted by the Department called for the Department to have 'a unified directing voice at a regional level' and has resulted in the creation of an internal Further Education and Higher Education and Employment (FEHEE) group which is planned to bring together all post-16 policy and operational policy into a single strategic centre within the Department (DfE 2022). This is taking further education in entirely the wrong direction and is absolutely contrary to the spirit of the Levelling Up White Paper which says it is committed to the principle of local growth policies. It reinforces centralization in policymaking when the real need is decentralization to regional authorities, which are close to the activities, both to create policy initiatives from the regions bottom-up but also to enable them to be coordinated more effectively with wider regional economic and social issues. Education is a critical element in a 'levelling up' process, though largely ignored in the White Paper but to be an effective change agent it needs to be very much more integrated with its localities and regions. The adoption of a tertiary system in England and decentralization from Whitehall would mark a fundamental step to the redressing of regional inequality.

Two important principles in respect to the governance of further education need to be protected. The first relates to the legal autonomy of the colleges, which after a shaky start back in 1993 when corporate status was conferred, has served the colleges well. Joining up with higher education in a tertiary system must not leave colleges at risk from domination by a larger and more prestigious university sector; their autonomy and freedom of action must be protected. Secondly, a move to tertiary should not discourage a continuation of a commitment to non-higher education professional programmes or to the kind of educational re-entry programmes run for example at Merthyr Tydfil College described in Chapter 4. The development of a tertiary system should be designed to offer the prospect of broadening colleges' missions not restrict them.

Assessing the value of regional engagement

We have seen in Chapter 6 how the governance of higher education has moved increasingly away from local and regional influence towards the centre. In a situation where 50 per cent of the relevant age group enters higher education and about half that attend institutions in their own region by choice, the extent of the public's involvement in the governance of the system in England is minimal: the OfS is a central regulator with no regional policy interests (its predecessor the Higher Education Funding Council for England (HEFCE) did at least appoint regional advisers); moreover, it is regarded as an arm of government. At the institutional level local or regional representation on governing bodies is reducing and being replaced by members drawn from a national pool, usually London-based, whose contribution is essentially that of a 'non-exec' on a company board. Democratic accountability at the regional level is almost non-existent. In its place, as in many other fields, we have a centralized bureaucracy reflecting metropolitan-based policies which have little purchase in the diverse picture of university engagement described in Chapters 2 and 5.

Where in Norway we see a political environment which is overwhelmingly in favour of evening up its hinterland with its metropolitan regions, what we see in the UK is a situation where both major political parties, especially in times of austerity, have increasingly taken steps to maintain the paramountcy of centralized decision-making, except in respect to devolution to Scotland, Wales and Northern Ireland (decisions affecting less than 15 per cent of the total UK population) and to the halting introduction in England of metro-mayors and Combined Authorities. One result of this central dominance is the extremes of inequalities that exist between and within the different regions as described in Chapter 1. These are restrained in Germany by the acceptance of the principle of the maintenance of homogenous living conditions embodied in constitutional law and its application by the *Länder* in the maintenance of a much less differentiated higher education system than can be found in the UK. The mood in the UK, and notably in England, is now more sympathetic to a programme of 'levelling up', but it is important that it should not replicate the position in Ireland, as described by Hazelkorn, of vocal support for decentralization and the establishment of regional machinery to support it but a retention of a Dublin-centric form of higher education governance and direction. The creation of Combined Authorities in England is a promising start but the extent of the devolved powers that they are assigned will be the true text of their effectiveness.

A second great argument for decentralization relates to the need to release local and regional initiative in implementing new ideas into the higher education system: the creation of a tertiary education system in Wales would never have been introduced without devolution and the two most striking examples of institutional innovation, the creation of the Highlands and Islands University in Scotland and the development of the University of Lincoln in England were both the product of local ideas and enterprise, the former by the region and the latter by the city of Lincoln. We rightly celebrate the research orientations of the metropolitan research universities but we do not give sufficient individual credit to the achievements of Birmingham City University in its identification with the needs of Birmingham or to Chester and Gloucestershire Universities for their successful transition from a mono-disciplinary character to becoming embedded regional institutions, or to Plymouth and Lincoln Universities for the way they have broken inter-sectoral boundaries to form extensive further education college networks as integral components of their institutional strategies. We give little or no public recognition to the value of students who, on graduation from their local or regional university, return to contribute to their own communities instead of moving to employment hot spots elsewhere. Decentralization would nurture the process further as well as facilitating more effectively than at present the interface between higher and further education.

Changes are afoot in Scotland and Wales. Decentralization would be a welcome stimulant to change in England; it would represent an essential step in the process of alleviating inequality but, in recognizing territorial identity, it would also add to the distinctiveness of the systems and the institutions they contained. We have attempted to show in Chapter 2 the extent to which locality and region has contributed to the formation and character of the individual communities, yet to their communities they are mostly viewed as national entities, only tangentially part of the local or regional environment. One does not need to go back as far as Hoggart's description of Leeds University in the 1930s as being 'part of the folklore and fabric of daily life' of the community (Hoggart 1988: 187) to think that a greater identification with regional concerns would be beneficial both for the public image of higher education and for individual institutions. We need a more bottom-up process of developing policy in higher education, and systems need to be more rooted in their communities than in the regulatory minutiae of a central command and control orientated centre. This does not mean that the state would lose control because it would remain responsible for research policy, would remain the custodian of quality assessment and would continue to require institutional accountability. Institutions themselves would retain their international profiles – there is no evidence to suggest that universities in Scotland and Wales have in any way dropped in international rankings – but they would gain strength from a closer integration with the activities of regional partners and communities.

The UK has not followed the path of designating categories of institutions to be universities of applied science as in Germany or Norway, or universities of technology as in Ireland as it could have done in 1992 or in relation to the establishment of the post-post-1992 universities. This was a good decision because it has reduced, if not removed, artificial divisions between types of institutions thus providing opportunities for greater institutional initiative and more flexibility in respect to institutional changes of mission: our evidence points to the fact that the Universities of Leeds and Newcastle are as committed to regional agendas as Chester and Gloucestershire but their contributions are of a different character. An important outcome of decentralizing higher education in England would be to redraw reputational weightings in a more regional context so that contributions to widening participation or regenerating communities were seen to be as valuable as capital intensive hubs aimed at generating new industries in inner-city locations. Decentralization to regions would introduce greater variety and flexibility into the management of higher education, increase institutional diversity and would offer an alternative perspective to traditional institutional hierarchies. It would also redraw the bonds, now much weakened, which link higher education institutions to their local and regional environments. If universities are to play their part in the modern world they need to draw more of their strengths and distinctiveness from local and regional sources rather than be seen as the manifestation of a centralized state whose policies are only tangentially aligned to local and regional needs.

References

Chapter 1

(1) UR 4.3.2
(12) UR 1.2.12

Chapter 2

(1) UR 3.1.2
(2) UR 3.3.13
(3) UR 4.3.3
(4) UR 2.2.9
(5) UR 2.2.9
(6) UR 3.6.2
(7) UR 4.7.13
(8) UR 4.5.11
(9) UR 2.2.12
(10) UR 2.5.2
(11) UR 2.1.3
(12) UR 2.1.4
(13) UR 2.3.9

Chapter 3

(1) UR 1.3.1
(2) UR 3.8.2
(3) UR 4.3.7
(4) UR 4.3.4
(5) UR 4.5.3
(6) UR 3.2.5

Chapter 4

(1) UR 3.4.11
(2) UR 3.8.11
(3) UR 3.8.4
(4) UR 3.9.4
(5) UR 3.9.7
(6) UR 3.9.9
(7) UR 3.9.6
(8) UR 2.1.4
(9) UR 3.9.10
(10) UR 4.3.8
(11) UR 4.3.8

Chapter 5

(1) UR 1.1.5
(2) UR 1.2.9
(3) UR 1.1.6
(4) UR 3.4.12
(5) UR 1.3.5
(6) UR 1.3.7
(7) UR 2.1.2
(8) UR 2.5.10
(9) UR 4.5.11

Chapter 6

(1) UR 2.1.5
(2) UR 3.1.6
(3) UR 4.3.6
(4) UR 3.4.6
(5) UR 4.5.8
(6) UR 4.1.6
(7) UR 2.2.6
(8) UR 1.3.4
(9) UR 2.4.3
(10) UR 2.1.8
(11) UR 3.4.7
(12) UR 4.1.7
(13) UR 3.2.9
(14) UR 1.3.5
(15) UR 3.6.7
(16) UR 3.1.6
(17) UR 1.1.5

Chapter 7 (7.1)

(1) N 3.6.9
(2) N 2.3.11
(3) N 1.9.5
(4) N.1.6.2
(5) N 1.10.9
(6) N 1.10.11
(7) N 2.3.12
(8) N.3.2.8
(9) N 3.6.3
(10) N 3.6.7
(11) N 2.2.16
(12) N 1.4.13
(13) N.2.3.4
(14) N 1.10.18

Works Cited

ARU Peterborough (2020), 'New £30 million university for Peterborough is officially launched by Universities Minister', retrieved from https://arupeterborough.co.uk/new-30-million-university-for-peterborough-is-officially-launched-by-universities-minister/

Back, H.J. and D. Furst (2011), 'Der beitrag von Hochschulen zur Entwicklung einer Regionals "Wissensregion"', E-paper der Arl. Verlag der Arl-Akademie für Raumforschung.

Barrett, D. (2018), *Dominant Cities in Small Advanced Economies: Challenges and policy responses*, retrieved from https://igees.gov.ie/wp-content/uploads/2019/03/Dominat-Cities

Barry, F. (2007), 'Third level education, foreign direct investment and economic boom in Ireland', *International Journal of Technology Management* 38 (3), 198–218

Bergin, A., E. Kelly and P. Redmond (2020), 'The Labor market in Ireland 2000–2018', *IZA World of Labor* 1–12, https://doi.org/10.15185/izawol.410.v2

Birmingham City University (2021), *2025 Strategy*, Birmingham: Birmingham City University.

Boland, T. (2009). 'Directed diversity – a strategy for the Irish Higher Education System for the 21st century', *Colloquium: World Class Universities or World Class University Systems*, Dublin: Dublin Institute of Technology.

Bleiklie, I. (2009), 'Norway from tortoise to eager beaver?' in C. Paradeise, E. Reale, I. Bleiklie and E. Ferlie (eds), *University Governance. Western Comparative Perspectives*, Dordrecht: Springer.

Bounds, A. (2021). 'Birmingham remakes itself as alternative to London', *Financial Times*, 20 April.

Bridge Group/UPP Foundation (2021), *Staying Local: Understanding the value of graduate retention for social equality*, London: UPP Foundation.

Britton, J., L. van der Eroc, B. Waltman and Nu Tiaowell (2021), 'The impact of living costs on the return to higher education', *IFS Research Study*.

Chaytor, S., G. Gottlieb and G. Reid (2021), 'Regional policy and R&D: Evidence, experiments and expectations', Oxford: Higher Education Policy Institute Report 137.

Clancy, P. (1995), *Access to College: Patterns of Continuity and Change*, Dublin.

Cochrane, A. and R. Williamson (2013), 'Putting higher education in its place: The socio political geography of English universities', *Policy and Policies* 41 (1): 43–58.

CoD (1993), *Technological Education – The Key to the Competitive Society*, Dublin.
CoD (2003), *Institutes of Technology and the Knowledge Society – Their Future Position and Roles. Report of the Expert Working Group*, Dublin.
Committee of Vice-Chancellors and Principals (CVCP) (the Jarratt Report) (1985), *The Report of the Steering Committee on Efficiency Studies in Universities*, London: CVCP.
Committee of University Chairmen (CUC 2020), *Higher Education Code of Governance*. London: CUC.
Costello, F. and E. Hazelkorn (2018), 'Assessing teaching and learning in Ireland' in H.P. Weingarten, M. Hicks and A. Kaufman (eds), *Assessing Quality in Postsecondary Education. International Perspectives*, Kingston, Ontario: School of Policy Studies, Queens University: 85–106.
CSO (2018), Population and Labor Projections 2017–2051 Population Projections Results 2017, retrieved from https://www.cso.ie/en.releasesandpublications/ep/p-plfp/populationandlaborforceprojections2017-2051/
Coyle, D. and M. Sensier (2020), 'The Imperial Treasury: Appraisal methodology and regional economic performance', *Regional Studies* 54 (3): 283–95.
Cullinan, J. and B. Halpin (2017), 'A spatial economic perspective on higher education choices' in J. Cullinan and D. Flannery (eds), *Economic Insights on Higher Education Policy in Ireland. Evidence from a Public System*, 53–80, Basingstoke: Palgrave Macmillan.
Day, N., C. Husbands and B. Kerslake (2019), *Making Universities Matter: How higher education can help to heal a divided Britain*, Oxford: Higher Education Policy Institute, Report 125.
Department for Education (2022), Review of the Education and Skills Funding Agency. Summary Findings, retrieved from https://assets.publishing.service.gov.uk/government/uploads/system/uploads/attachment_data/file/1054696/Review_of_the_Education_and_Skills_Funding_Agency_summary_findings.pdf
Department of Jobs, Energy and Industry (2014), a. Table of Actions, retrieved from https://enterprise.gov.ie/en/Publications/Publication-files/2014ap1-Table-of-Actions.pdf
Department of Jobs, Energy and Industry (2014), Background Paper, Strategy for Science, Technology and Innovation 2015–2020, Dublin.
Donnelly, M. and S. Gamsu (2018), 'Home and away: Social and spatial inequalities in student mobility', The Sutton Trust, Bath: University of Bath.
Drucker, J. and H. Goldstein (2007), 'Assessing the regional economic development impacts of universities: A review of current approaches', *International Regional Science Review* 30: 20–46.

Duff, T., J. Hegarty and M. Hussey (2000), *The Story of the Dublin Institute of Technology*, Dublin: Blackhall Publishing.

Feldman, M.P. (2000), 'Location and innovation: The new economic geography of innovations, spill overs and agglomeration', in G.L. Clark, M.P. Feldman and M. Gerther (eds), *The Oxford Handbook of Economic Geography*, Oxford: Oxford University Press.

Fritsch, M. (2009), 'Was konnen Hochschulen zur regionalen Entwicklung beitragen?' *Die Hochschulen*, 1/2009: 39–52.

Garmendia, A. (2021), 'The political determinants of decentralisation', in I. Largo (ed.), *Handbook of Decentralisation, Devolution and the State*, 91–115, Cheltenham: Edward Elgar Publishing.

Giovannini, A (2021), 'The 2021 metro-mayors' elections: Localism re booted', *The Political Quarterly* 92 (3): 474–85.

Goddard, J. and P. Vallance (2013), *The University and the City*, Abingdon: Routledge.

Goddard, J., E. Hazelkorn, L. Kempton and P. Vallance (eds) (2016), *The Civic University: The policy and leadership challenges*, Cheltenham: Edward Elgar Publishing.

Government of Ireland (1967), *Steering Committee on Technical Education. Report to the Minister for Education on Regional Technical Colleges*, retrieved from https://assets.gov.ie/24673/b639a1eac94642a0a839ea32bb9a7779.pdf

Government of Ireland (1992), *Regional Technical Colleges Act, 1992.*

Government of Ireland (1997), *Universities Act 1997.*

Government of Ireland (2018a), *National Development Plan 2018–2027*, retrieved from https://www.gov.ie/pdf/?file=https://assets.gov.ie/37937/12baa8feOdcb43a78122fb316dc51277.pdf#page=null

Government of Ireland (2018b), *National Planning Framework*, retrieved from https://www.gov.ie/en/policy-information/07e507-national-development-plan-2018-2027/

Government of Ireland (2018c), *Project Ireland 2040. Building Ireland's Future*, retrieved from https://asets.gov.ie?7335/7692660a70b143cd92b1c65ee892bo5c.pdf

Government of Ireland (2018d), *Technological University Act 2018. Pub.L.No Number 3 of 2018.*

Hale, T. and A. Bounds (2019), 'The Manchester model', *Financial Times*, 4 June.

Hardiman, T. P., M.J. MacCormack, R.E.D. Bishop, O.H.G. Marenholtz, D.T. Wright and M. Gleeson (1987), *Technological Education. Report of the International Study Group to the Minister for Education*, Dublin.

Hazelkorn, E., A. Gibson and S. Harkin (2015), 'From massification to globalization: Reflections on the transformation of Irish higher education', in K. Rafter and M. O'Brien (eds), *The State in Transition: Essays in honour of John Horgan*, 235–60, Dublin: New Island Books

Hazelkorn, E. and A. Moynihan (2010), 'The challenges of building research in a binary higher education culture', in S. Kyvik and B. Lepori (eds), *The Research Mission of Higher Education Institutions Outside the University Sector*, https://doi.org/10.1007/978-1-4020-9244-2

Higher Education Authority (2011), *Regional Clusters, Consolidation Leading to Mergers, Strategic Dialogue*, Dublin.

Higher Education Authority (2012), *Towards a Future Higher Education Landscape*, retrieved from https://hea.ie/assets/uploads/2017/04/Towards-a-Higher-Education-Landscape.pdf

Higher Education Authority (2013), *Report to the Minister for Education and Skills on System Reconfiguration, Institutional Collaboration and System Governance in Irish Higher Education*, retrieved from https://www.education.ie/en/Publications/Policy-Reports/HEA-Report-to the Minister-for-Education-and Skills on Irish higher education.pdf

Higher Education Authority (2020), *Graduate Outcomes Survey Class of 2018*, retrieved from HEA website: https://hea.ie/assets/uploads/2020/06/HEA-Graduate-Outcomes-Survey-Class-of2018 pdf

Higher Education in the Learning Society, *National Committee of Inquiry into Higher Education* (NCIHE) (the Dearing Report) (1997), London: HMSO.

Higher Education Strategy Group (2011), *National Strategy for Higher Education to 2030*, retrieved from Department of Education and Skills, Government of Ireland, http//.hea.ie/files/DES_Higher_Ed_Main_Report.pdf

Hinfelaar, M (2012), 'Emerging higher education strategy in Ireland: Amalgamate or perish', *Higher Education Management and Policy* 24 (1): 1–16.

H.M. Treasury (2021), *Building Back Better: Our plan for growth*, London: CP 401 March.

Hochschulrahmengesetz (1998), *Tekst des Hochschulenrahmengestz in der Fassung des vierten Gesetzes zur Anderung des Hochschulenrahmengesetzes vom 20 August 1998*. BGBl 1S. 2190: Bonn.

Hochschulrektorenkonferenz (2016), *Die Hochschule als zentrale Akteure in Wissenschaft und Gesellschaft* (Senatsbeschluss der Hochshulrektorenkonferenz vom 13.10.2016), HRK: Berlin.

Hoggart, R. (1988). *A Local Habitation*, Oxford: Oxford University Press.

Hooghe, L. and G. Marks (2016), *Community, Scale and Regional Governance: A Postfunctionalist theory of governance*, Vol. II, Oxford: Oxford University Press.

Huggins, R., P. Thompson and D. Prokop (2019), *UK Competitive Index 2019*, Cardiff: Cardiff University School of Geography and Planning/Notting Business School.

Ives, E., D. Drummond and L. Schwarz (2000), *The First Civic University: Birmingham 1880–1980*, Birmingham: University of Birmingham Press.

Jones, W., R. Moseley and G. Thomas (2010), *University Continuing Education 1981–2006: Twenty-five turbulent years*, Leicester: National Institute of Adult Continuing Education.

Kelly, U., D. McLellan and I. Nichol (2016), *Making an Economic Impact: Higher education and the English regions*, London: Universities UK.

Kollydas, K. and A. Green (2022), 'Graduate pathways: Identifying patterns of regional development and attraction', West Midlands Regional Economic Development Institute/City-Region Economic Development Institute, Birmingham.

Krücken, G. (2003), 'Mission impossible? Institutional barriers to the diffusion of the third academic mission at German universities', *International Journal of Technology Management* 25 (1–2): 18–33.

Kujath, H.J., P. Pasternack and V. Radinger-Peer (2019), 'Governance-formen des regionalen Wissen-transfers', in R.-D. Postlep, L. Blume and M. Hulz (eds), *Hochschulen und ihr beitrag für eine nachhaltige Regionalentwicklung*, 76–118, Hanover: Forschungsberichte der ARL 11–Akademie für Raumforschung und Landesplannung.

Kyvik, S. and B. Stensaker (2013), 'Factors influencing the decision to merge – the case of strategic mergers in Norwegian higher education', *Tertiary Education and Management* 19 (4): 323–37.

Ladner, A., N. Keufer, H. Baldersheim, N. Hlepas, P. Swianiewicz, K. Steyvers and C. Navarro (2019), *Patterns of Local Autonomy in Europe*, London: Palgrave Macmillan.

Landtag Mecklenburg-Vorpommern (2015), Eckwerte der Hochschulentwicklung 2015–2020. Schwerin: Drucksache 6/4033.

Levelling Up in the United Kingdom (2022), Policy Paper CP 604, London.

Lisauskaite, E., S. McIntosh, S. Speckesser and H. Espinoza (2021), 'Going further, further education, disadvantage and social mobility', Sutton Trust/Centre for Vocational Education Research.

London Higher (2021), www://londonhigher.ac.uk/civic map

Loughlin, J., F. Hendriks and A. Lidstrom (eds) (2011), *The Oxford Handbook of Local and Regional Democracy in Europe*, Oxford: Oxford University Press.

Maassen, P., E. Moen and B. Stensaker (2011), 'Reforming higher education in the Netherlands and Norway: The role of the state and national modes of governance', *Policy Studies* 32 (5): 479–95.

McCann, P. (2019), 'Perceptions of regional inequality and the geography of discontent: Insights from the UK', *Regional Studies* DOI 10.1080/00343404,2019,1619928.

MacFeely, S. (2016), 'Opportunism over strategy: A history of regional policy and spatial planning in Ireland', *International Planning* Studies 21 (4): 377–402, https://doi.org/10.1080/13563475.2016.1162403

McMahon, F. (2008), 'Technical education, technical colleges and further education in Ireland', in P. Elsner, G. Boggs, and J. Irwin (eds) *Community Colleges, Technical Colleges and Further Education Programmes*, retrieved from http://arrow.dit.ie/cgi/viewcontent.cgi?article=1001&context=diraabk&sei-redir=1&referer=http://scholar.google.co.uk/scholar?q=issues+in+apprenticeships+ireland&hl=en&btnG=Search&as_sdt=1%2C5&as_sdtp=on#search=%22issues apprenticeships

Marginson, S. (2012), *Criteria for Technological University Designation. Prepared for the Department of Education, Government of Ireland*, retrieved from http://www.cit.ie/contentfiles/Marginson reportcriteria+for+technological+university+designation+final.pdf

Melville, D. and D. Macleod (2000), 'The Present Picture', in A. Smithers and P. Robinson (eds), *Further Education Reformed*, 26–37, London: Falmer Press.

Ministry of Housing, Communities and Local Government (2019), *The English Indices of Deprivation 2019*, London: HMSO.

Morgan, J. (2021), 'Local partnerships bridge HE-FE divide', *Times Higher Education*, 24 June: 17.

Morgenroth, E.L.W. (2008), *Exploring the Economic Geography of Ireland* (No. 271), Dublin: Economic & Social Research Institute.

Morgenroth, E.L.W. (2018), *Prospects for Irish Regions and Counties: Scenarios and Implications*, Dublin: Economic & Social Research Institute.

Morgenroth, E.L.W. and J. Fitzgerald (2006), *Ex Anti Evaluation of the Investment Priorities for the National Development Plan 2007–2013*, retrieved from https://www.esri.ie/system/files/media/file-up;oads/2015-07/JACB200613.pdf

Mulcahy, N., T. Dunphy, C. McCarthy, E. McDermot and J. Sheehan (1967), *Steering Committee on Technical Education Report to the minister for Education on Regional Technical Colleges*: 10, retrieved from https://assets.gov.ie/24673/b639aleac94642aOa839ea32bb9a7779.pdf

Newcastle City Council, Newcastle University, Legal and General (2020), *Newcastle Helix: A new home for innovation and business in the centre of Newcastle*, Newcastle.

OECD (2006), *Reviews of National Policies for Education – Higher Education in Ireland*, https://doi.org/10.1057/9781137289889

OECD (2007), *Higher Education and Regions: Globally competitive, locally engaged*, Paris: OECD.

Piggot, V. (2020), Ireland enrolment and graduate 5-year trends, retrieved from https://hea.ie/2020/07/03enrolement-and-graduate-5-year-trends/

Postlep, R.-D. and L. Blume (2019), 'Governance-formen des regionalen Wissentransfers', in R.-D. Postlep, L. Blume and M. Hulz (eds), *Hochschulen und ihr Beitrag für eine nachthaltige Regionalentwicklung*, 76–118, Hanover: Forschungberichte der ARL 11– Akademie für Raumforschung und Landesplanung.

Quin, B. (2014), 'Resources and resourcefulness: Ireland and EU regional policy' *Administration* 62(2): 25–45.

Radinger-Peer, V., G. Pflitsch, T. Freytag and T. Doring (2019), 'Transformationprozesse im Hochschulsystem in Richtung nachhaltige Regionalentwicken ('Empirische Illustrationen') in R.-D. Postlep, L. Blume and M. Hulz (eds), *Hochschulen und ihr Beitrag für eine nachhaltige Regionalentwicklung*, 177–207, Hanover: Forschungsberichte der ARL 11— Akademie für Raumforschung und Landesplanung.

Schakel, A.H. (2021), 'Exploring and explaining trends in decentralisation', in I. Largo (ed.) *Handbook of Decentralisation, Devolution and the State*, 27–52, Cheltenham: Edward Elgar Publishing.

Schubert, T. and H. Kroll (2013), *Endbericht zum Projekt 'Hochschulen als regionaler Wirtschaftsfaktor'*, Auftrag von Stifterverband für die Deutsche Wissenschaft, Karlsruhe: ISI.

Schuller, T., J. Preston, C. Hammond, A. Basset-Grundy and J. Brynner (2004), *The Benefits of Learning: The impacts of education on health, family life and social capital*, London: Routledge-Falmer.

Shattock, M.L. (2012), *Making Policy in British Higher Education 1945–2011*, Maidenhead: McGraw-Hill/Open University Press.

Shattock, M.L. and A. Horvath (2019), *The Governance of British Higher Education: The impact of governmental, financial and market pressures*, London: Bloomsbury Academic.

Shattock, M.L. and A. Horvath (2020), 'The decentralisation of the governance of UK higher education: The effects of devolution on Scotland, Wales and Northern Ireland, and on England', *Policy Reviews in Higher Education*: 164–78.

Shattock, M.L. and S. Hunt (2021), 'Intersectoral relationships within higher education: The FE/HE interface in the UK', Centre for Global Higher Education Working Paper No. 70.

Skillbeck, M. (2001), *The University Challenged: A review of international trends and issues with particular reference to Ireland*, Dublin: HEA.

Smithers, A. and P. Robinson (2000), 'Introduction: The Making of a New Sector' in A. Smithers and P. Robinson (eds), *Further Education Reformed*, 1–13, London: Routledge/Falmer Press.

Sorber, N. (2018), *Land Grant Colleges and Popular Revolt*, Ithaca: Cornell University Press

Staton, B. (2021), 'Manchester link up to boost industry', *Financial Times*. 3 June

Stensaker, B. (2014), 'Troublesome institutional autonomy. Governance and the distribution of authority in Norwegian universities', in M.L. Shattock (ed.), *International Trends in University Governance*, 34–49, Abingdon: Routledge.

Swinney, P. and M. Williams (2016), *The Great British Brain Drain: Where graduates move and why*, November, Centre for Cities.

The 2070 Commission (2020), *Make No Little Plans: Acting at scale for a fairer and stronger future,* https://uk2070.org.uk/wp-content/uploads/2022/06/Declaration-of-Intent-Brochure.pdf

Thorn, R. (2018), *No Artificial Limits: Ireland's regional technical colleges*, Dublin: Dublin Institute of Public Administration.

Trow, M. (1974), 'Problems in the transition from elite to mass higher education', *Policies for Higher Education*, Paris: OECD.

Tselios, V. (2021), 'Federalism and income inequality' in I. Largo (ed.) Handbook of *Decentralisation, Devolution and the State*, 270–87, Cheltenham: Edward Elgar Publishing.

TU4Dublin (2013), *Consultation on Successor to the Strategy for Science, Technology and Innovation 2006–2013*, retrieved from https://enterprise.gov.ie/en/Consultations/consultation-files/Technological-university-for Dublin.pdf

TURN (2019), *Technological Universities, Connectiveness and Collaboration Through Connectivity. Report of the Technological Universities Research Network to the Department for Education and Skills*, retrieved from https://assets.gov.ie/39280/174b686cce5741a896c7264fed7edfd9.pdf

UPP (2019), *Truly Civic: Strengthening the connection between universities and their places,* London: UPP.

Valero, A. and J. van Reenen (2016), *The Economic Impact of Universities: Evidence from across the globe*, NBER Working Paper 22501.

Webb, J., M. Johns, E. Roscoe, A. Giovannini, A. Quereshi and R. Baldwin (2022), *The State of the North 2021–2022 Powering Northern Excellence*, IPPR North.

Whitburn, J., M. Mealing and C. Cox (1976), *People in Polytechnics*, London: Society for Research in Higher Education.

Willetts, D. (2017), *A University Education*, Oxford: Oxford University Press.

Wissenschaftsrat (2010), *Empfehlungen zur Rolle der Fachhochschulen im Hochschulsystem*, Berlin: WR.

Wissenschaftsrat (2016), 'Wissens- und Technoligietransfer als Gegenstand institutioneller', Strategien Positionpaper, Weimar: WR.

Wissenschaftrat (2018), 'Empfehlungen für die regionale Kooperation zwischen wissenschaftlichen Einrichtungen', Weimar: WR.

Zhang, Q. C. Larkin and B.M. Lucy (2017), 'The economic impact of higher education institutions in Ireland: Evidence from disaggregated input-output tables', *Studies in Higher Education* 42 (9): 1601–23 https://doi.org/10.1080/13075079.2015.1111324

Index

The letter *f* after an entry indicates a page with a figure.

accountability 134–5
adult education. *See* extra mural studies
anchor institutions 5–6
apprenticeship degrees 67

Benefits of Learning, The (Schuller, T. et al.) 41
Birmingham 20, 21
Birmingham City University 142
    engagement strategies 68–9
    graduate locations 44*t*
    local industry, relationships with 65
    region 20–1, 33
    student recruitment 33, 37*t*
Bishop Grosseteste University 24
Blackpool and The Fylde College 56
Bridge Group study 42–3
Bruntwood 17
Buchanan Report 99–100
Building Back Better: Our plan for growth (H.M. Treasury) 16–17, 18
business R&D expenditure 14*f*–15

Cardiff University 138
centralization 76, 77–8, 140–1
    England 124
    European comparators 124–30
    Ireland 96–7, 124, 125, 128
    Norway 124, 125, 126, 128
    tertiary education system 123
    UK 126, 127, 129, 141
Cheltenham and Gloucester College 22
cities 16–19
    innovation hubs 17–18, 20, 21, 39–41, 56, 65–6, 74, 85, 114
    investment in 17, 39–41
City College Coventry 48
City Deals 17
city regions 6

civic universities 2–3, 38 *see also* Russell Group universities
    autonomy 75
    founding 75
    funding 76
    institutional governance 75
Clothworkers Company 61
CNAA (Council for National Academic Awards) 127
Cochrane, A. 1
colleges *see also* further education
    universities, collaboration with 48–59
Combined Authorities 6, 12, 31, 32, 63, 65, 132, 135–6, 141
community regeneration 41, 42
commuter universities 34
competitiveness 13
    The UK Competitiveness Index 13
Council for National Academic Awards (CNAA) 127
Coventry 48
Coyle, D. 15
Crosland, Tony 47

De Montfort University 77
Dearing Committee Report 77
decentralization 4, 6, 47–8, 123–43
    England 4, 48, 130–6, 142–3
    European comparators 124–30
    functional logic 132
    further education 139–40
    Germany 124, 125, 126, 127, 136
    identity logic 132–3
    Northern Ireland 131
    partial 133
    principles 133–5
    Scotland 130, 131
    UK 124, 127, 129, 130–1

university autonomy 136–9
Wales 130, 131
Department of Education and Science (DES) 62, 64
deprivation 15, 40–3
  English Indices of Deprivation 13
  Gloucester 22
  Lancaster University region 26, 33, 55–6
  Merthyr Tydfil 52–3, 54
  Newcastle University region 32, 67
  University of Chester region 23
  University of East London region 21
  University of Plymouth region 23–4
  University of Stirling region 26, 33
devolution 4, 6, 126, 129, 130–1, 132, 141
differentiation 2, 7
diversity 1–2, 19, 110
Donnelly, M. 30, 40

education *see also* further education *and* higher education
  inadequate 41
  local 29, 30, 33, 34, 36, 37t, 38, 42, 43
  tertiary 123–43
Ellesmere Port 23
Enders, Jurgen 125, 129
engagement strategies 65–72
England 129–30, 139
  centralization 124
  decentralization 4, 48, 130–6, 142–3
  further education 48
  further/higher education collaboration 56–7
  tertiary education 130–6
  university autonomy 137
equality 124–5 *see also* inequality
  Germany 114–15, 130, 141
  Norway 124, 125, 130, 141
executive, the 78, 79, 82, 83, 85, 86
  Ireland 98
  Norway 91–2
extra mural studies 62–4

FEHEE (Further Education and Higher Education and Employment) group 140
Forth Valley College 56
funding 57–8, 76, 135
  Germany 113–14, 116, 117
  extra mural studies 62–4
  UK 2, 47, 61, 76, 126
further education 139–40
  autonomy 140
  college/university interface 49–51
  decentralization 47–8, 139–40
  in deprived communities 52–3, 54, 55–6
  higher education, relationship with 47–9
  institutional governance 140
  interface management 56–9
  planning 62
  pre-1992 universities and colleges 55–6
  universities, collaboration with 48–59
  university/college network structures 51–4
Further Education and Higher Education and Employment (FEHEE) group 140
Further Education Funding Council 47

Gamsu, S. 30, 40
Germany 107–19, 129, 130
  Bologna Process 113, 116–17, 129
  collaborations 117
  constitutional provision for equality between regions 114–15, 130
  decentralization 124, 125, 126, 127, 136
  equality 124–5, 141
  funding 113–14, 116, 117
  German Science Council 112, 113, 119
  graduate locations 116–17
  higher education, relationship with region 108–11
  Innovative Higher Education 114
  institutional governance 107, 109, 110, 113, 115, 117–19, 124
  Länder, the 107, 109, 110, 113, 115, 117, 119, 124, 127, 133, 141
  levelling up 114–15, 130, 141
  massification 107, 109, 110, 119
  Region Innovative programme 114
  regional engagement, recent trends 111–15
  structurally weak areas 114–15, 130
  student recruitment 116–17
  technology transfer centres 111

tensions/dilemmas 115–17
tertiary education 124
universities of applied science
    (*Fachhochschulen*) 108, 109–10, 113,
    114, 116, 117, 119, 124, 127, 129,
    130, 136
university autonomy 11, 136
Giovannini, A. 132
Gloucestershire 22–3
Goddard, John 1
*Governance of British Higher Education.
    The impact of governmental,
    financial and market pressures*
    (Shattock, M. and Horvath, A.) 4,
    130
governing bodies 78–86
graduate locations 40, 41, 42–5, 97–8,
    116–17, 142
graduate outcomes 39–46
    graduate locations 40, 41, 42–5, 97–8,
        116–17, 142
    salaries 40
Great British Brain Drain, The (Centre for
    Cities) 16, 17
Green, A. 40

Hazelkorn, Ellen 125, 141
HEIF (Higher Education Innovation
    Fund) 62
higher education *see also* universities
    college/university interface 49–51
    further education, relationship with
        47–9
    interface management 56–9
    planning 62
    pre-1992 universities and colleges 55–6
    university/college network structures
        51–4
Higher Education Innovation Fund
    (HEIF) 62
Highlands and Islands Enterprise 25
Hoggart, Richard 38–9, 45, 142
Horvath, A. 77, 130
Huggins, R. 13
human capital 41, 42, 45
Hunt, S. 49

identity capital 41
identity logic 132–3

industrial decline 15
industry, relationships with 61, 64, 65, 69,
    70, 71, 73
inequality 13–16, 49, 54, 141 *see also*
    equality *and* levelling up
    pockets of 15
    UK 125
innovation hubs 17–18, 20, 21, 39–41, 56,
    65–6, 74, 85, 114
institutional governance 75–8, 134, 140–1
    business model 77
    centralization 76, 77–8
    civic universities 75
    executive, the 79, 82–3
    further education 140
    Germany 107, 109, 110, 113, 115,
        117–19, 124
    Norway 91–3, 94–5
    polytechnics 77
    practice 78–82
    regional engagement 78–86
intersectorial interface 47–59
Ireland 96–107, 129, 130, 141
    Buchanan Report 99–100
    centralization 96–7, 124, 125, 128
    Dublin 96, 97, 100, 106
    Dublin, concentration of universities
        in 97, 106, 125
    economy 97, 99–100
    European Economic Community 99,
        100
    graduate locations 97–8
    Higher Education Authority 128
    higher education policy changes 101–3
    institutional mergers 128 9
    linking regions and higher education
        105 7
    massification 98, 102
    National Spatial Strategy 100
    population 97
    Project Ireland 2040 100, 104, 106
    regional policy 99–101
    Regional Skills Fora 106
    regional structures 100, 102–3
    smart specialization agenda 105, 106
    student recruitment 97, 98
    technical colleges 101–2
    tertiary education system 123–4
    TURN report 104, 105

Universities of Technology/
  technological universities 98, 102,
  103–6, 129
university autonomy 137

Jarratt Committee report 76–7

Kollydas, K. 40
Krücken, G. 111

Lancaster University 31
  colleges, collaboration with 55–6
  engagement strategies 67–8
  graduate locations 44*t*
  region 26, 27, 32–3
  student recruitment 33, 37*t*
lay members (of governing bodies) 78–81, 83–5
Leeds 66
Legal & General 17
LEPs (Local Enterprise Partnerships). *See* Local Enterprise Partnerships
levelling up 7–8, 16–17, 41, 84, 135, 140
  England 130, 141
  Germany 114–15, 130, 141
  Norway 124, 125, 130, 141
  tertiary education system 123
  University of Lincoln 36
Levelling Up the United Kingdom 8, 17
Lews Castle College of Further Education Stornoway 54
local authorities, relationships with 61–2
Local Enterprise Partnerships (LEPs) 10, 85
  funding 135
  Lancaster University 26
  Newcastle University 66
  University of Chester 23, 70
  University of East London 34
  University of Gloucestershire 22–3, 36, 70
  University of Leeds 32, 65
  University of Lincoln 25, 52
London 132
  affluence 21
  deprivation 21
  employment dominance of 16
London Higher Civic Map 131–2

McCann, P. 13
Making an Economic Impact: Higher Education and the English Regions (Kelly, U., McLellan, D. and Nichol, I.) 1
Manchester
  Innovation District project 17–18
Manchester Metropolitan University 18
massification 98, 102, 107, 109, 110, 119, 126
Merthyr Tydfil College 52–3
metro mayors 6, 12, 132
Ministry of Housing, Communities and Local Government 13

National Strategy for Higher Education to 2030 (Higher Education Strategy Group) 102
NEETs (Not in Education, Employment or Training) 53
New Universities 2–3, 37–8
  STEM subjects 72
Newcastle Helix 39–40, 66
Newcastle University 31, 39, 143
  colleges, collaboration with 55
  engagement strategies 66–7
  graduate locations 44*t*, 45
  local industry, relationships with 65
  Newcastle Helix 39–40, 66
  region 19–20, 32
  research 138
  student recruitment 32, 37*t*
Newham 21
NEXUS enterprise and innovation centre 65
NHS 73, 74
NIFU (Nordic Institute for Studies in Innovation, Research and Education) 93, 94
NOKUT (Norwegian Agency for Quality Assurance in Education) 88, 90, 91, 128, 136 Nordic Institute for Studies in Innovation, Research and Education (NIFU) 93, 94
Northern Ireland 130–1, 138
Northumbria University 66
Norwegian Agency for Quality Assurance in Education (NOKUT) 88, 90, 91, 128, 136

Norway 87–96, 129, 130
  centralization 124, 125, 126, 128
  Councils for Cooperation with
    Working Life 93–5, 96, 128, 137
  equality between regions 124, 125, 130,
    141
  higher education system,
    regionalization in 88–9
  institutional governance 91–3, 94–5
  institutional mergers 88, 89, 90, 91, 92,
    93–4, 128
  levelling up 124, 125, 130, 141
  Ministry of Education and Research
    89–90, 92
  NOKUT 88, 90, 91, 128, 136
  Quality Reform agenda 88, 91–2, 93, 95
  regional dimension 90–1
  system governance 89–90
  tertiary education system 123–4
  universities of applied science 88, 90
  university autonomy 89, 92, 93–5, 128,
    136–7
nursing 52–3

Office for Students 141
OfS 141

PCAS (polytechnics and colleges
  admission system) 29
Peterborough 40
polytechnics 3, 30, 47, 127
  local authorities, relationships with 62
  institutional governance 77
  centralization 77
  student recruitment 30–1
polytechnics and colleges admission
  system (PCAS) 29
Polytechnics and Colleges Funding
  Council 47
post-1992 universities 3, 127
  colleges, collaboration with 49–50
  funding 14
  institutional governance 78
  local authorities, relationship with 62
  local industry, relationships with 65, 73
  STEM subjects 72–3
  student recruitment 33–5, 37–9, 50
post-post-1992 universities 3, 127
  colleges, collaboration with 49–50, 59

  engagement strategies 69
  funding 14
  local industry, relationships with 73
  STEM subjects 72, 73
  student recruitment 35–6, 37–9, 50
post-2000 universities. *See* post-post-1992
  universities
pre-1992 universities
  colleges, collaboration with 49–50,
    55–6
  extra mural studies 62–3
  institutional governance 75, 78
  local industry, relationships with 61, 65
  student recruitment 31–3, 37–9, 50
Prince Charles Hospital 53
public sector, relationships with 65, 72–4

QAA (Quality Assurance Agency) 134
Quality Assurance Agency (QAA) 134

REF (Research Excellence Framework)
  133
regional development 61
regional engagement 61–5
  Germany 107–19
  industry, relationships with 61, 64, 65,
    69, 70, 71, 73
  institutional governance 78–86
  Ireland 96–107
  NHS 73, 74
  Norway 87–96
  public sector, relationships with 65,
    72–4
  STEM subjects 72–3
  strategies 65–72
  value of 140–3
regional inequality 13–16
regions 7 *see also* regional inequality
  administrative 6
  cities and 16–19
  city regions 6
  definition 6–7
  environment 3–4, 5
  graduate locations 44*t*
  regeneration 5
  student recruitment 29
  universities and 19–27
  university-defined 6–7
research 16, 61–2, 67, 138

funding 3, 14–15, 16, 133–4
  Germany 113, 114, 116
Research Excellence Framework (REF) 133
research-led universities 64
Russell Group universities 2, 14, 49–50, 55, 72 *see also* civic universities

Schakel, A.H. 132
Schuller, T. et al. 41
Shattock, M. 49, 77, 130
science and technology 3, 17, 72–3
Scotland 4, 130
  decentralization 4, 48, 130, 131, 137–8
  further education 48
  university autonomy 137–8
Sensier, M. 15
Seven Sisters universities 2
Siemens 71
social capital 41, 42
social class 29–30, 38
STEM subjects 72–3
Stensaker, B. 136–7
student recruitment 16, 29–37t, 48
  Germany 116–17
  international 34
  Ireland 97, 98
  post-1992 universities 33–5, 37–9, 50
  post-post 1992 universities 35–6, 37–9, 50
  pre-1992 universities 31–3, 37–9, 50
  Russell Group universities 55

teaching-led universities 14, 64–5 *see also* post-1992 universities *and* post-post-1992 universities
tertiary education 123–43
  England 130–6
  European comparators 123–30
  further education 139–40
  university autonomy 136–9
  Wales 4, 8, 47, 120, 139
Troublesome Institutional Autonomy: Governance and the distribution of authority in Norwegian universities (Stensaker, B.) 136
Truly Civic: Strengthening the connection between universities and their places (UPP) 5

Tselios, V. 133
tuition fees 57–8, 72, 76
TURN report 104, 105

UCAS (Universities and Colleges Admissions Service) 29
UCCA (Universities Central Council of Admissions) 29
UCG (University Grants Committee) 2, 47, 61, 76, 126
UK 129, 143
  centralization 126, 127, 129, 141
  decentralization 124, 127, 129, 130–1
  devolution 4, 6, 126, 129, 130–1, 132, 141
  equality 125
UKRI (United Kingdom Research and Innovation) 133
UMIST (University of Manchester Institute of Science and Technology) 18
United Kingdom Research and Innovation (UKRI) 133
United States 2
universities *see also* university autonomy
  as anchor institutions 5–6
  categories 143
  colleges, collaboration with 48–59
  commuter 34
  contribution of 1
  councils 75, 76, 77, 78
  courts 75, 77, 85
  dual intensive 26
  engagement strategies 65–72
  foundations of 2–3, 19
  funding 2
  local authorities, relationships with 62
  local industry, relationships with 61, 64
  location of 2, 3
  regions and 19–27
  research-led 64
  senates 78
  teaching-led 64–5
Universities and Colleges Admissions Service (UCAS) 29
Universities Central Council of Admissions (UCCA) 29

university autonomy 12, 47, 136–9, 140
   civic universities 75
   Germany 11, 136
   Ireland 137
   Norway 89, 92, 93–5, 128, 136–7
   Scotland 137–8
   Wales 137–8
university councils 75, 76, 77, 78
university courts 75, 77, 85
University Grants Committee (UGC) 2, 47, 61, 76, 126
University of Birmingham
   region 20
University of Chester 6, 59, 142, 143
   colleges, collaboration with 52
   courses 35
   engagement strategies 70
   graduate locations 44t, 45
   local industry, relationships with 70
   region 22, 23, 35–6
   student recruitment 35, 37t
University of East London
   engagement strategies 68
   graduate locations 44t–5
   local industry, relationships with 69
   region 21–2, 34
   student recruitment 34, 37t
University of Edinburgh 138
University of Glasgow 138
University of Gloucestershire 6, 59, 142, 143
   engagement strategies 70
   graduate locations 44t, 45
   region 22–3, 36
   student recruitment 36, 37t
University of Leeds 6, 31–2, 39, 142, 143
   Clothworkers Company 61
   engagement strategies 65–6, 67
   extra mural studies 63
   founding 75
   graduate locations 44t, 45
   Hoggart, Richard 38–9
   local industry, relationships with 65
   region 19–20, 31–2
   research 138
   student recruitment 32, 33, 37t, 38–9
University of Lincoln 6, 59, 142
   colleges, collaboration with 51
   engagement strategies 71–2
   graduate locations 44t, 45
   local industry, relationships with 71
   region 24–5, 36
   student recruitment 36, 37t
University of London 55
University of Manchester 17–18, 138
University of Manchester Institute of Science and Technology (UMIST) 18
University of Plymouth 6, 142
   colleges, collaboration with 51–2, 59
   engagement strategies 68–9
   graduate locations 44t, 45
   local industry, relationships with 65, 69, 73
   region 23–4, 34
   student recruitment 34–5, 37t
University of Salford 18
University of South Wales 6, 15
   colleges, collaboration with 52–4
   engagement strategies 68–9
   graduate locations 44t
   local industry, relationships with 69, 73
   region 24, 35
   student recruitment 35, 37t
University of Stirling 31
   colleges, collaboration with 56
   engagement strategies 67, 68
   graduate locations 44t
   region 26–7, 32, 33
   student recruitment 33, 37t
University of Sunderland 66
University of the Highlands and Islands 4, 6, 40, 142
   colleges, collaboration with 54
   engagement strategies 70–1
   graduate locations 44t, i45
   region 25–6, 36–7
   student recruitment 37t
university senates 78
Uses of Literacy, The (Hoggart, Richard) 38

Valero, A. 109
Van Reenen, J. 109
vice-chancellors 78, 79, 83

Wales 4, 14, 130, 133, 141
   decentralization 4, 47–8, 130, 131, 137–8
   further education 47–8
   further/higher education collaboration 56–7
   tertiary education 4, 8, 47, 120, 139
   university autonomy 137–8
Whitburn, J. 29, 30, 31
Willetts, D. 41
Williamson, R. 1

www.ingramcontent.com/pod-product-compliance
Lightning Source LLC
Chambersburg PA
CBHW052126300426
44116CB00010B/1799